Presented To:

_____

From:

_____

Date:

_____

THE
KINGDOM
AT
WAR

DESTINY IMAGE BOOKS BY ALAN VINCENT

The Good Fight of Faith

Heaven on Earth

THE
KINGDOM
AT
WAR

USING INTERCESSORY PRAYER
TO DISPEL THE DARKNESS

ALAN VINCENT

DESTINY IMAGE₍ᵣ₎ PUBLISHERS, INC.

P.O. Box 310, Shippensburg, PA 17257-0310

"Promoting Inspired Lives."

This book and all other Destiny Image, Revival Press, MercyPlace, Fresh Bread, Destiny Image Fiction, and Treasure House books are available at Christian bookstores and distributors worldwide.

For a U.S. bookstore nearest you, call **1-800-722-6774.**

For more information on foreign distributors, call **717-532-3040.**

Reach us on the Internet: **www.destinyimage.com.**

ISBN 13 TP: 978-0-7684-4066-9

ISBN 13 Ebook: 978-0-7684-8898-2

For Worldwide Distribution, Printed in the U.S.A.

1 2 3 4 5 6 7 8 / 15 14 13 12 11

DEDICATION

TO my wife, Eileen, my companion in the warfare, so wonderfully feminine, but a mighty warrior; and to my three children and their outstanding children along with them. I dedicate this book to this next generation of warriors emerging in the Church.

THANKS

FIRST, I want to thank God that this project is completed. It was some years ago that the first seeds for the manuscript were revealed to me. Now with the finished book in my hand, I must express my thanks to all who have been part of this project. Every book is something of a joint effort, and this one is no different.

My thanks overflow to the Lord, who has so wonderfully helped me to write, even in a very busy life. I am especially grateful for the encouragement from my wife, Eileen, who has helped me to keep going. The editing was accomplished by Margie Knight, Natalie Hardy, and Eileen Vincent.

We also wish to express our thanks to Destiny Image Publishers. They have been so accommodating and encouraging. It is a pleasure to interact with them.

Endorsements

As Alan Vincent sets out in *The Kingdom at War*, he effectively re-prioritizes the Kingdom of God. He then gives us the training insights necessary to engage present-day principalities and powers from our position as "seated with Christ in heavenly places." Our destiny as Kingdom citizens is to bring glory to our King. Father promises that His glory *will* fill the earth. As the Body of Christ, we bring Him glory individually and corporately by being transformed into the image of Christ who is Love *(Agape)*. It is in *Agape* that we will see signs and wonders and miracles—the power to transform and reform the pillars of our present-day society. This author clearly shows us what the Church needs to do, apart from the encumbrances of religious tradition. *The Kingdom at War* will, in my opinion, contribute greatly to our seeing the Kingdom revealed in power and glory.

Bob Mumford
Lifechangers
Bible Teacher and Author of *The King and You, Dr. Frankenstein and World Systems, Agape Road,* and *Mysterious Seed*

This book expresses Alan Vincent's heart—the Kingdom of God impacting our cities and nations in a tangible, practical way. I have had the privilege of walking with Alan Vincent as a son for more than 20 years and know his desire for building "spiritual cities" and raising up churches and ministries with the characteristics of the "tabernacle of David." The book you hold in your hand explains both of these concepts, the biblical foundation and the practical implementation of the revelation that Alan has carried for the way the Church in our cities should function. I have also had the privilege of implementing a measure of this teaching in various cities and seeing it work. Please do take time and study what Alan teaches here; it will change your city and/or nation.

Franz Lippi
Founder and Leader, B.L.A.S.T. Ministries
(Balkan Loving Apostolic Serving Team)
Graz, Austria

CONTENTS

FOREWORD

APOSTLE Alan Vincent is more than a great man of God whom I greatly admire and respect. He has the theology, revelation, and personal experience of the Kingdom. He is an authority on this subject. He took the Kingdom to Bombay, India, and today, he shares the divine revelation on how to prepare for the coming of the Kingdom of God, how to bring it to Earth, and how to see the glory of God invade the natural realm. He also teaches how to experience the flow of miracles—a rare occurrence in today's society.

One important revelation you will find in *The Kingdom at War* is on new wine and new wineskins. I can testify that implementing his teachings on this subject, with the revelation and demonstration of the Kingdom, have been instrumental in the continual growth of our church. I am a witness as to how the revelation and demonstration of the Kingdom can establish the sovereignty and Lordship of the King of kings, Jesus!

I love and appreciate Apostle Alan Vincent for his practical teachings, which I am certain will bless you and lead you into a deeper understanding of the war we face against the kingdom of darkness. His wisdom on this subject will take you into a higher dimension of revelation and demonstration of the Kingdom of God.

Dr. Guillermo Maldonado
Apostle and Cofounder,
King Jesus International Ministry
Miami, Florida

INTRODUCTION

PREPARATION FOR THE COMING OF THE KINGDOM

THE longer I live and dig into God's wonderful Word, the more I marvel at the revelation that the prophets (particularly Isaiah and Jeremiah) received in their day. I am amazed at the way they were able to look down the centuries, way beyond their own time, and see the unfolding and relentless purposes of God. The vision God showed Isaiah started in his day, moved down through hundreds of years to the birth of Jesus our Savior, and continues on to the end of the age.

Isaiah was first called to prophesy in the year that King Uzziah died. This king, as a young teenager, turned the nation of Judah back to God with great enthusiasm and restored many from their backslidden ways. In Uzziah's younger years, under the tutelage of the prophet Zechariah, God gave Judah great victories over their enemies and prospered them abundantly. The reformation under Uzziah's leadership moved in the right direction. However, it stopped short of God's full standard, because he did not remove the high places, which were still being used to worship other gods.

In later years, because of his great economic and military successes, Uzziah became proud and inflated with his own importance. He even tried to enter the temple to burn incense like the high priest did, but he was prevented from doing so by the Levitical priests. God immediately struck him with leprosy for his presumption; soon after that, he died in isolation after 52 years as king. Just as Uzziah fell into sin, the nation of Judah backslid again into witchcraft and the worship of other gods.

In the year King Uzziah died, Isaiah was called to become God's prophet. At that time, Isaiah had an awesome vision of the Lord in the temple. As God visibly filled the place with His presence and His glory, Isaiah melted in His presence, becoming acutely aware of his own unclean lips and the unclean lips of all God's people. (See Isaiah 6:1-6.)

In Isaiah 7:14 we read his remarkable prophecy regarding the virgin birth of Jesus:

> *Therefore the Lord Himself will give you a sign: Behold, the virgin shall conceive and bear a Son, and shall call His name Immanuel* [which means God with us].[1]

In Isaiah 9:6-7, he further announced:

> *For unto us a Child is born, unto us a Son is given...His name will be called Wonderful, Counselor, Mighty God, Everlasting Father, Prince of Peace. Of the increase of His government and peace there will be no end. Upon the throne of David, and over His kingdom, to order it and establish it with judgment and justice from that time forward, even forever. The zeal of the Lord of hosts will perform this.*

In between these two Scriptures, as we look back at Isaiah 8:10-21, we read of the dark and difficult days in Judah during which Isaiah was prophesying. God was no longer being honored, revered, or sought after by His people. Instead, every kind of witchcraft and occult activity, including openly consulting witches and seeking the dead, was being practiced. As a result, a thick spiritual darkness covered the land. It could be speaking of much of the present-day United

States, Western Europe, and the rest of the world, which is tragically in a similar condition.

Isaiah looked to God as his only hope and waited to hear what He had to say and what He would do about this appalling situation. God's response at that time was to speak directly to him of the coming Messiah and declare in Isaiah 8:18:

> *Here am I and the children whom the LORD has given Me! We are for signs and wonders in Israel from the LORD of hosts who dwells in Mount Zion.*

This glorious passage is quoted again in Hebrews 2:13 and is directly attributed to Christ Himself.

God's answer was to declare His intention of using His own true children as human agents on Earth to overpower the devil in every way with a mighty manifestation of the supernatural power of God.

These signs and wonders demonstrated through His children would spearhead the breakthrough, but had to be accompanied by God-fearing holiness, humility, and purity of life in His servants. They would also establish proper government so the transforming authority and the peace of the Kingdom of God could be properly established and continue increasing until it finally filled the earth.

If we want to see the Kingdom of God established in our day and continue to increase, if we desire to see His government established in our cities and the power of Jesus and His Kingdom spreading over the whole earth, then we must cry out for mighty signs and wonders to be done in His name.

God is still passionate about this, just as He promised Isaiah, saying: "...*The zeal of the Lord of hosts will perform this*" (Isa. 9:7). God's government and God's peace always work hand in hand. For these reasons, this book is devoted to equipping you to:

1. Discover how to move in the power of signs, wonders, and
    miracles—which has always been God's way of announcing

and establishing His Kingdom and the main means of obtaining the initial breakthrough—while maintaining a holy environment which allows this power to continue to flow.

2. Participate in establishing a proper spiritual government within the Church so that the Kingdom may go on increasing until it invades and transforms every pillar of our society.

3. Engage in effective spiritual warfare against the principalities and powers in heavenly places, resulting in the casting down of these demonic strongholds.

4. Identify the role of God's angels in these last days and how they will work together with the apostles, the prophets, and other God-appointed generals and soldiers in the Lord's Army.

5. Recognize and abandon all religious traditions that would hinder the coming of the Kingdom in all its power and glory.

6. Create and become a new, flexible wineskin that can hold the power and thrust of this Kingdom's "New Wine" without either the wine or the wineskin being spoiled.

We are living in perilous, yet exciting times, and I pray that the biblical principles set forth in this book will prepare you to walk into your God-ordained calling and destiny.

ENDNOTE

1. *Biblesoft's New Exhaustive Strong's Numbers and Concordance with Expanded Greek-Hebrew Dictionary.* CD-ROM. Biblesoft, Inc. and International Bible Translators, Inc. (© 1994, 2003, 2006); s.v. "Immanuw'el," (OT 6005).

CHAPTER 1

THE GLORY OF THE KINGDOM
INVADING THE WORLD

DURING our initial ministry years in the early 1960s, my wife Eileen and I served as missionaries in Bombay, India (now known as Mumbai). At that time, God began preparing a small group of us who were desperately hungry for a move of God to be His instruments of change. He used us to break through the demonic darkness and forcefully invade that community with the transforming power of the Holy Spirit, thereby ushering in the glory of His Kingdom. This story is told in the first chapter of my previous book on the Kingdom, titled *Heaven on Earth.*[1]

A permanent transforming experience occurred in me during that time while spending 21 days praying and meditating over every word in Paul's letter to the Ephesians from 1:1 through 2:8 until these truths became part of my very being. The small group of us who took part in this exercise came to fully embrace the revelation that we could actually live the risen life of Jesus by faith, in spite of our circumstances.

We, first of all, had to learn how to corporately and individually live by grace through faith so that the power of His glorious resurrection life could be manifested in us on a continual basis. These realities became part of us, along with the wonderful words of Jesus in His final discourse with His disciples as recorded for us in John 13–17. Through the revelation of the Spirit, we came to understand the rights and authority God had already given us in Him in this life, providing we fulfilled the conditions of loving the Father and obeying Him in everything just as Jesus had done throughout His life on Earth.

Just like Paul, we needed to learn how to "sit down" with and in Jesus on His mighty throne, which was already situated in the heavens far above all principalities and powers in the lower heavens (see Eph. 2:4-7). From that position, He taught us how to exercise rule in His name over all the demonic forces that had already established themselves in the heavenly realm. We were then ready and able to deal with them and cast them down; we were also able to overcome all the demonic forces that opposed us and attacked us on Earth.

DEPLOYING THE KING'S AIR FORCE

It is futile for us to attempt to advance the Kingdom by spiritual warfare and limit ourselves to fighting only at the earthly level. To be effective, we must, as a first priority, learn how to invade the heavenly realm and deal with the demonic principalities and forces already established there.

To fail to do this would be like an army trying to win a war using only ground troops without the assistance of air power. In a modern military battle, to refrain from using strategic air power would be a crazy military strategy. No army would try to advance through a valley with only tanks and foot soldiers; nor would the military fail to call on its air force to first target and remove enemy gun positions located up in the hills on either side of the valley. If they tried to advance without doing this first, the enemy guns on higher ground would rain down artillery shells on their advancing troops and cause heavy casualties.

Unfortunately, that is exactly what much of the Church has been doing for a long time—failing to deploy the King's Air Force, which is an essential part of spiritual warfare. She has been far too earthbound. She has not seen her full potential or known how to exercise her heavenly air power effectively in the heavenly realm. It is only when we learn to remove those demonic principalities in heavenly places by strategic spiritual warfare that we will begin to see the breakthrough on Earth.

That is why we are going to look at the essential elements of spiritual warfare in this book. To achieve this, we need to observe and understand the structure of the strongholds of the kingdom of darkness that are already established. With this valuable intelligence in play, we can learn how to overcome them more effectively.

SATAN'S STRONGHOLDS IN THE HEAVENS

Shortly after their creation as man and woman, Adam and Eve made the tragic decision to believe the devil's lies and step out from under God's loving and benevolent rule into an independent life of their own. They thought they were stepping out into a life where they would be self-governing and self-emancipating and would, by their own effort, increasingly become like God. They expected to remain free from sin *and* become like God by using the resources of their own moral power. But instead, once they stepped out into independence, they and their descendants immediately came under the devil's merciless control. Sin came into the world; then, through people, the devil began to establish his own rebellious kingdom on Earth.

God did not immediately bring the deserved judgment upon the devil and humanity. Instead, because He loved Adam and Eve, God decided to redeem them and all their descendants and recover all that they had lost by sending His own Son, Jesus, to die for them on the cross. But this also meant that God, in His perfect righteousness, could not bring judgment to the devil and his angels without judging Adam and his descendants at the same time. So He allowed Adam to continue as His delegated authority on Earth and also allowed the devil to continue his activity on Earth while the process of humanity's salvation was still being worked out.

To establish his own kingdom on Earth, satan has to work through people and use them as his delegated authority, just as God had done when He first created Adam and Eve and gave them rule over all that He had created on Earth. If satan cannot continue to deceive humankind and bring them under his power, whether consciously or unconsciously, then he cannot maintain his evil kingdom of darkness, fear, and death on Earth.

The Bible teaches us that the demonic influence keeping so many people captive in satan's kingdom here on Earth is a spiritual power that emanates from a polluted heavenly realm. Therefore, to be able to advance the Kingdom of God, we must learn to deal with that heavenly realm and cleanse it from all its demonic strongholds and controlling influences.

Then, when this is accomplished, many lost people will suddenly have their eyes opened to see *"the glory of God in the face of Jesus Christ"* (2 Cor. 4:6). They will be convicted of their sin, cry out for mercy, repent and turn to the Lord, and joyfully come under His authority. As a result, they will be totally set free from satan's power.

Satan's kingdom has a hierarchical structure of arch-demons who lead hordes of rank-and-file demons that willingly serve satan under his headship. We meet two of these in the Book of Daniel. They are called the prince of Persia and the prince of Greece (see Dan. 10:20).

As soon as Daniel began to pray for the prophetic words of Jeremiah and Isaiah to be fulfilled, violent warfare broke out in the heavens. This was because Daniel's prayers were invading that heavenly realm and giving God's archangels, Michael and Gabriel, and their army of loyal angels, the legal opportunity to attack and cast down the princes of Greece and Persia.

Because of these warring prayers, Daniel was so strongly attacked spiritually by these agents of satan that the demonic pressure almost crushed him. So Gabriel was sent by God to strengthen Daniel and urge him to keep praying.

His prayers were an essential part of God's strategy to throw down these evil spiritual powers, thereby fulfilling God's prophetic Word and bringing about the final victory (see Dan. 10:1-20).

WINNING THE LEGAL BATTLE

In *Heaven on Earth,* I discussed the prayer life of Jesus in Luke's Gospel and briefly explained the parable of the persistent widow in which Jesus taught His disciples the need to first get a legal victory before actually going to war against demonic powers.

When someone begins to pray as Jesus taught in Luke 18:1-8, things begin to happen in the heavenly realm. Spiritually speaking, we must first learn how to fight and win these "legal battles" before we engage in the full-scale "military battles" that necessarily follow. These military battles begin when a group of intercessors actually goes to war against demonic powers in the heavenly places with the purpose of casting them down.

If we try to fight the military battle before we have won the legal battle, we make it very difficult for ourselves.

When we fight military battles, numbers are critical, but when we fight the corresponding legal battles, one person praying alone can be enough. You don't even need two.

In this parable from Luke 18, Jesus taught His disciples that even one frail widow was enough—providing she was willing to persist until she got a favorable verdict from the Judge of the highest court, which is the court of Heaven where Jesus sits with all power and authority.

I can now see that this is what happened to us years ago in Mumbai. The Spirit of God taught my wife, Eileen, and me how to fight and win that kind of legal battle so that the ruling spirit over that region of our city finally had to leave. Thankfully, there were two of us, but it could have been done by only one.

Omar Cabrera, a great Argentinean prayer warrior and evangelist, power-fully demonstrated this principle in the early days of the Argentinean Revival by single-handedly taking on and casting down the ruling demon in a number of cities in Argentina. Once he had accomplished this, he saw a tremendous break-through in a number of cities. Many people were converted, and large churches were established. I remember hearing this great pioneer tell the story personally to me about 40 years ago.[2]

This parable in Luke 18:1-8 was given by Jesus to teach us that we should always persist in prayer and never faint or lose heart due to opposition or delay. He especially seemed to emphasize this as being necessary as the day when His return draws near.

One of the puzzling things about this kind of spiritual warfare praying is the long delay we sometimes experience before we see any answers to our prayers. From our perspective, it seems like God is not very interested in the thing we are praying about, or else He seems powerless or unwilling to do anything about it. That is not the truth at all, but from our perspective, it sometimes seems like it is. In actuality, something is being wrestled through in the spirit realm, and it is absolutely essential that we stay in the heavenly courtroom pleading our case until God can give us the final verdict in perfect righteousness.

Jesus taught two stories on persistent prayer: One is in Luke 18:1-8; the other is in Luke 11:1-10. Each story teaches us to understand a different principle.

In Luke 18:1-8 we are taught that an unrighteous judge who does not fear God and who is not a bit interested in bringing justice can still be made to do the right thing. Although he doesn't care about the request being made to him, but is corruptly more concerned about his own power and financial benefits, righteousness can prevail. Jesus taught that if we persist in our appeals to God, who is the Righteous Judge, the corrupt officer will be forced, despite his own desires, to do the right thing. We see this being worked out when Paul appeared before Gallio, the proconsul of Achaia in Corinth (see Acts 18:12-18) and the city clerk in Ephesus (see Acts 19:34-41).

We are also learning to do this effectively in the cities of different nations in which we presently work.

ASKING A FRIEND FOR A FRIEND

In Luke 11:1-4, in what is usually called "The Lord's Prayer," Jesus taught that we must first of all have effective prayer lives of our own so as to get our personal needs met. But that is only stage one. Jesus then immediately asked (in verse 5) whether we are willing to go a stage further in prayer and learn how to appropriate answers to prayer on behalf of our friends.

Eileen and I first learned this lesson in Mumbai, and it moved us into the real spirit of prayer and intercession. Because of the desperate needs all around us, we constantly found ourselves praying for the needs of others. We learned how to obtain healings from all kinds of sicknesses and diseases and also saw numerous people wonderfully delivered from alcoholism. We helped obtain jobs for unemployed people and homes for people who had nowhere to live. We became experts in these prayers.

As a result, we never had any long-term unemployment in our church despite constant high unemployment in the city. Just as the economy of God's people in Goshen was different from the economy of Egypt, so the economy of the Kingdom is different from the economy of the world. Through this, God taught us some important lessons. Sometimes He deliberately delayed answers in order to train us in persistence and to develop our spiritual muscles. But all this was only preparation. He was getting us ready for the real spiritual warfare that lay ahead.

REASONS FOR DELAY IN ANSWERED PRAYER

I believe there are four reasons why God sometimes deliberately delays answers to prayer when we pray for our friends in need.

First, He uses the delay to train and strengthen us in our persistence in prayer. In this way, we are prepared and strengthened for the real spiritual warfare that is still ahead.

Second, He sometimes uses delay to purify our motives. A wife may earnestly pray for her unconverted husband, saying, "Oh God, save my husband."

God may then ask, "Why?"

She may have to get honest and confess: "Because I can't stand him the way he is, and he would be much nicer to live with if he became a Christian!" Her true concern is not about his salvation, but the unpleasantness of his unsaved state.

Sometimes people pray for their cities with similar motivations, because they selfishly desire a nicer city in which to live. They are asking for the right thing, but for the wrong reason. It is not really the burden of lost souls or the many needy people that motivates them. It's their personal enjoyment and comfort that mainly concerns them. Sometimes, a purification of our motives in prayer is required, and the answers are delayed until we begin praying for the right things for the right reasons.

Third, delay often sharpens the focus of our prayers. Many people came to Jesus with very general requests: "Oh, Lord, help me!" "Please Lord, do something!"

Every time people spoke that way to Jesus, He would ask them, "What exactly do you want Me to do for you?" He made them become very specific. Only then was He willing to answer their prayers (see Luke 18:35-42).

Fourth, we must pray in faith. Jesus and all the New Testament writers taught that our prayers must be prayers of faith without any doubt. We must trust the certainty that God will answer us, providing we pray according to His will (see 1 John 5:14-15).

Sometimes our prayers are only prayers of hope, not faith. We are thinking, "Well, let's ask Jesus, and see if He is able and willing to help us; but in case He doesn't answer, we'll try some other things at the same time and hope that one of them will work." If there is not real faith, there cannot be true persistence. But if we come to Him desperately in real faith, certain that He alone has the power and will do what we ask of Him, then we will receive whatever we ask.

A man once came to Jesus with a demonized son saying, "Lord, if You can do anything, please, help me" (see Mark 9:22).

Jesus threw the question straight back at him by saying, "If I can do anything? If *you* can really believe! All things are possible to those who believe" (see Mark 9:23). The real problem was not Jesus' ability or willingness to heal, but rather the man's unbelief.

Sometimes God deliberately uses delay to perfect our asking and develop our spiritual faith muscles. In some people, God's deliberate delay only develops a growing determined persistence. It may be driven initially by desperation, but it finally becomes a real prayer of faith that must be answered. A great example in Scripture is the persistent Canaanite woman with a demonized daughter. She would not let go till she got an answer and made even Jesus marvel at her faith (see Matt. 15:22-28).

PRAYER TACTICS OF SPIRITUAL WARFARE

When we enter into real spiritual warfare, as we read in Luke 18, we are no longer praying to our Friend in Heaven for things our earthly friends may need. We have an adversary, the devil, who has come against us and is attacking us and seeking to do us harm or even destroy us. In such instances, we want vengeance—or more literally, we want our "legal rights" over him, because there is mutual enmity between him and us!

Once again, we find Jesus describing an unrighteous judge who doesn't seem to be bothered about justice. Instead, he just wants this pesky widow-woman to stop bothering him all the time. Notice again that there has to be persistence because through our faith-filled, persistent prayer, we can actually force unrighteous officials to do God's righteous will when they don't even realize it.

It is not really because of indifference on God's part that there is a long delay even though, from our point of view, He sometimes seems to behave indifferently. As Jesus goes on to explain in Luke 18:6-8:

> *Hear what the unjust judge said. And shall not God avenge His own elect who cry out day and night to Him, though He bears long with them? I tell you that He will avenge them speedily. Nevertheless, when the Son of Man comes, will He really find faith on the earth?*

In fact, the Greek text explains more fully that God is passionately and earnestly waiting for the necessary righteous procedures to be completed so He can then act speedily on our behalf. Legions of angels are available to God and eager to help His saints on Earth, but they need to be released legally. If we fight and win these legal battles first and get a successful verdict from God, the Righteous Judge, then these angels can be released by Jesus to come and help us when the actual conflict with the demonic hosts begins. If we do not first win the legal battle to get these good angelic hosts righteously released to help us, we end up fighting enraged demons on our own without angelic help. This is not the best way to fight, and we will probably lose the battle.

This little widow had a strong adversary who sought to do her much harm, and she wanted vengeance against him because she was convinced of her legal rights. Jesus did not paint a picture of some strong, self-confident James Bond kind of individual; instead, He chose for His illustration a single, weak widow-woman who had a legally legitimate case against her adversary, but no power to enforce it. She knew her legal rights without any doubt, so she wouldn't give up.

What Jesus said in this parable is that it does not matter how small or weak you are. It does not matter how seemingly insignificant you are. If you learn how to pray and are sure of your legal rights based on what Jesus accomplished through the cross, and if you persist like this woman did, then you will get powerful answers to your prayers. You will defeat all the demonic powers in the heavenly realm over your city if you simply persist.

These legal battles can be won by just one person. You can pray for your city on your own and be the instrument that causes the Father to release powerful angels to change that city. This widow had no influence, no money, and no power. All she had was persistence and real faith; but that was enough to get an answer.

If we are asking for the throwing down of a powerful demonic adversary, we have to go first of all to the courts of Heaven where the risen Christ sits on His mighty throne with all power and all authority. As plaintiffs, we have to be born of God and have learned by faith to sit down with Christ on His heavenly throne. We must know that we have authority to reign with Christ. We must believe that in Jesus' name we have a legal right to plead the case and take possession of the city on behalf of Jesus and His Kingdom.

It does not matter how small or weak you are. As long as you are that kind of person, you can become a legitimate legal intercessor for your city. Because of your legal standing as a redeemed child of the King, the case will be heard in Heaven before God's throne. The Spirit of God will show you how to pray and how to plead the case for your city (see Rom. 8:26-27). The Scriptures tell us that Jesus lives to make intercession for us (see Heb. 7:25). God, the Righteous Judge, is already on your side, but He cannot give you the verdict just because He loves you. He will, however, answer you speedily once your case is proven to be legal and righteous.

As he battles in the heavenly places, the devil attempts to present counter-arguments as to why he should not be thrown out of the city. During this time, he might come and attack you by trying to intimidate you so as to stop you from praying. He will attack you with doubt and depression. If you don't persevere until the judgment is given, even if you have a perfectly valid case, you will lose your case.

Many Christians start praying for a legitimate cause, but they don't persevere until the answer comes. With persistent and persevering praying, the answer may suddenly come even after many years of waiting. Its suddenness may surprise you. In my first book on the Kingdom I told about our situation in

Mumbai. The breakthrough suddenly happened one Wednesday night after years of praying and battling. The ruling demonic principality was cast down; everything changed, and from that day the city was different.

If you persist, a day will come when the Judge will rule on your behalf. When that happens, He will legally and righteously be able to release many angels to enforce the judgment that has been given. They will come and fight with you. Oh, how they are longing and waiting for believers who will press through and open the way for them to legally enter into the battle! Then you become workers together with angels as well as with God, and what a beautiful and mighty thing it is when that happens!

THE MILITARY BATTLE

Once the verdict has been obtained, the next phase is the enforcement of what has been judicially granted to you. When you come to the enforcement stage, you don't just stay in the prayer room. You take to the streets and go into action. You work together with other saints and learn to cooperate with angels to make glorious and wonderful things happen all over the city for which you have been praying.

This is what I call the military phase. It is when we go and cast out demons, heal the sick, and loose people from all their demonic bondages. Drug addicts, alcoholics, and prostitutes, as well as many respectable, ordinary people, turn to the Lord. The members of drug cartels and violent gangs are converted or leave town, and peace comes to the city. You shut down the sex shops and close the abortion clinics and, physically, you begin to change the feel and very appearance and function of your city. Corruption is cleansed from every aspect of public life, and then you see righteous and godly government established.

At this stage, numbers really count, so the more people you can muster, the better. According to Jesus' words, many angels are available in groups of thousands, and they are ready to go! They are longing for us to pray for our cities so that they can be legally released to come and do the work of God's Kingdom in partnership with us. But the military phase cannot effectively come until the legal phase has been successfully accomplished.

By nature, most humans are activists and not pray-ers. A common mistake made by churches is to go out too soon in a flurry of activity without the divine mandate to validate what they are doing. There are no fighting angels available because they have not yet been legally released to come and help. You don't want to find yourself in the position of fighting on your own. It's tough, and you won't see any results. When you do that sort of thing on your own initiative, little happens.

This often produces discouragement in individuals and churches. Some will give up the fight and back away, which is exactly what the devil wants to see happen. The people may have responded well at the start; but when nothing really changes, they are slow to respond a second time, because of deep disappointment. As a result, it becomes much harder to rally the people to try another evangelistic thrust. To get them to go out a second or third time is hard work, if not virtually impossible. It is so important to do the right things, in the right way, at the right time, and in the right order.

But if you organize real, God-directed, evangelistic activity in which many are being healed and saved and all of your people are being used and are seeing results, your people will not get bored or tired at all. They'll be absolutely thrilled. When angels are working all over the city and you just go and work *with* them, it's exciting and stimulating. When you actually see the harvest being reaped, it is exhilarating; you feel like you could joyfully do this for the rest of your life.

CHANGING THE POLITICAL MAP

In the Book of Daniel, we find Daniel wrestling in prayer. He was praying for a nation to be delivered from captivity and for God's prophetic word concerning Judah to be fulfilled. God had already said through the prophet Jeremiah that after 70 years His people would be released from captivity and would return to their own land (see Jer. 25:9-12). At the end of Isaiah chapter 44 and into the beginning of chapter 45, Isaiah named the person through whom God would bring about this deliverance. He was a pagan king named Cyrus who didn't even know God. Nevertheless, God said he would be His instrument.

Daniel began his lonely prayer warfare possibly with only his three friends praying with him. It was a prayer battle that lasted more than 70 years. Daniel went into captivity as a teenager in 608 B.C. and prayed for almost 50 years (until 559 B.C.) before anything happened. Then Cyrus became the king of Persia. At that time Persia was not a particularly powerful nation, but I can imagine Daniel asking God, "Is this the man that Isaiah spoke about?" And God replying, "Yes, this is the man! Now I want you to promote him politically with your prayers."

That is something we need to learn to do. We cannot transform cities without getting the right politicians, civic leaders, and judges into place. We must either change the hearts of the present politicians to fear God or, by the power of our prayers, replace them with those who do. As a result, they will start working with us and not against us. We must pray for the right men and women to become more prominent, influential, and powerful while we also pray for the wrong people to lose their prominence and influence.

Wherever you live, remember also to pray for your national politicians, state politicians, and your capital city as well as those in your own city, because this will greatly affect what you are able to do there.

Whoever was on the throne of the Persian-Median Empire in Sushan, the capital city, politically determined what would happen in the city of Jerusalem more than 1,000 miles away. Getting the right people in the right political positions is a powerful and important part of taking cities for the Kingdom. Ezra records how the temple was rebuilt successfully through the prayers and prophesying of God's prophets, the activity of His apostolic leaders such as Nehemiah, and the cooperation and commandments of the three secular kings Cyrus, Darius, and Artaxerxes (see Ezra 6:13-16).

Daniel's prayer life was the key for a whole nation to be released from captivity. In some remarkable scriptural passages, Jeremiah had prophesied:

Therefore thus says the LORD of hosts: "Because you have not heard My words, behold, I will send and take all the families of the north," says the LORD, "and Nebuchadnezzar the king of Babylon, My servant, and will bring them against this land, against its inhabitants, and against these nations all around, and will utterly destroy them, and make them an astonishment, a hissing, and perpetual desolations. Moreover I will take from them the voice of mirth and the voice of gladness, the voice of the bridegroom and the voice of the bride, the sound of the millstones and the light of the lamp. And this whole land shall be a desolation and an astonishment, and these nations shall serve the king of Babylon seventy years. Then it will come to pass, when seventy years are completed, that I will punish the king of Babylon and that nation, the land of the Chaldeans, for their iniquity," says the LORD; "and I will make it a perpetual desolation. So I will bring on that land all My words which I have pronounced against it, all that is written in this book, which Jeremiah has prophesied concerning all the nations" (Jer. 25:8-13).

For thus says the LORD: After seventy years are completed at Babylon, I will visit you and perform My good word toward you, and cause you to return to this place. For I know the thoughts that I think toward you, says the LORD, thoughts of peace and not of evil, to give you a future and a hope. Then you will call upon Me and go and pray to Me, and I will listen to you. And you will seek Me and find Me, when you search for Me with all your heart. I will be found by you, says the LORD, and I will bring you back from your captivity; I will gather you from all the nations and from all the places where I have driven you, says the LORD, and I will bring you to the place from which I cause you to be carried away captive (Jer. 29:10-14).

Isaiah had also prophesied saying:

Thus says the LORD, your Redeemer, and He who formed you from the womb: "I am the LORD, who makes all things, who stretches out the heavens all alone, who spreads abroad the earth by Myself; who frustrates the signs of the babblers, and drives diviners mad; who turns wise men backward, and makes their knowledge foolishness; who confirms the word of His servant, and performs the counsel of His messengers; who says to Jerusalem, 'You shall be inhabited,' to the cities of Judah, 'You shall be built,' and I will raise up her waste places; who says to the deep, 'Be dry! And I will dry up your rivers'; who says of Cyrus, 'He is My shepherd, and he shall perform all My pleasure, saying to Jerusalem, "You shall be built," and to the temple, "Your foundation shall be laid."'

Thus says the LORD to His anointed, to Cyrus, whose right hand I have held—to subdue nations before him and loose the armor of kings, to open before him the double doors, so that the gates will not be shut: "I will go before you and make the crooked places straight; I will break in pieces the gates of bronze and cut the bars of iron. I will give you the treasures of darkness and hidden riches of secret places, that you may know that I, the LORD, who call you by your name, am the God of Israel. For Jacob My servant's sake, and Israel My elect, I have even called you by your name; I have named you, though you have not known Me. I am the LORD, and there is no other; there is no God besides Me. I will gird you, though you have not known Me, that they may know from the rising of the sun to its setting that there is none besides Me. I am the LORD, and there is no other..." (Isa. 44:24–45:6).

Israel's release from captivity was promised in Scripture; nevertheless, Daniel didn't just sit down in his favorite chair and passively wait saying, "I'm just going to watch and wait for God to do His sovereign will and fulfill His Word all by Himself without my active involvement." No! The written prophetic word of Scripture became the target and the motivation for his prayer and all his activity.

He knew exactly what to pray because God told him what to pray. When he saw a king named Cyrus come to the throne of Persia, he was not a particularly powerful or prominent king. But Daniel recognized him as God's man and began to pray to promote him politically. Through Daniel's prayers, Cyrus then conquered Media and became the king of the Persian-Median Empire. Over the next 20 years, Cyrus went on to conquer Syria and then Assyria. He continued to grow in power and stature until he became the most dominant political force in the world apart from the king of Babylon. Finally, Babylon was conquered by Cyrus in 539 B.C., just one year short of the 70 years prophesied by Jeremiah. This set the stage for the prophetic words of Jeremiah and Isaiah to be fulfilled right on time.

In the first year of his rule over Babylon, Cyrus was stirred by the Lord in a dream to send all willing Jews back to Israel to rebuild the temple in Jerusalem. He sent back all the golden artifacts that were removed when Nebuchadnezzar destroyed the temple. Cyrus ordered that the costs of rebuilding the temple should be paid out of the royal treasury.

While this prayer battle was going on, Daniel was feeling such pressure and heaviness that he almost gave up. But because Daniel's persistent praying was so important to God's strategy, He sent the angel Gabriel to strengthen him. The case was being heard in the heavenly courtroom, but the judgment had not yet been given. If Daniel had stopped praying, the case could not have been completed, nor the demonic spirits thrown down.

CONTENDING WITH REGIONAL SPIRITS

The prince of Greece and the prince of Persia were two great demonic powers ruling over large regions of the world on behalf of satan, and they were in this fight along with all their hosts of demons.

The archangel Michael was in warfare against them along with Gabriel and a host of God's loyal angels. This was the fight of fights in Daniel's day. Gabriel briefly left the battle and came to Daniel to strengthen him. In essence he said, "Daniel! Don't stop praying! You must hang in there, son! Your prayers legitimize our activity in the heavens to bring down these demonic powers and cause the Word of God to come to pass."

Through Gabriel's visit, Daniel was strengthened to stick in there and pray till the victory came. These great demonic principalities were unable to withstand the prayers of this one God-empowered man. Through him God was able to legally enforce His Word. The right politicians came to the throne, and they started to work with God and His angels to bring about the restoration of the ruined city. But many more battles still lay ahead.

By this time, Daniel was well into his 80s or even early 90s. It was his prayers that produced the right political environment so that God's people were released to start rebuilding the temple right on time in 538 B.C.

Four years went by and the opposition from the surrounding enemies against the rebuilding became more and more intense. The people of God lost heart and were basically saying, "Man, I'm tired. I don't think this is the time to try to rebuild God's house. Why try to do something so ambitious? Besides, I have a few things to finish in my own house. It's not as comfortable as I would like it to be."

So they left the house of God in order to build more comfortable homes for themselves. Then the sympathetic and God-fearing King Cyrus was replaced by a renegade son named Cambyses II who repealed the political permission and removed the government funding they had been receiving to rebuild the temple in Jerusalem. So everything stopped in 534 B.C.

Do you know what also happened in 534 B.C.? Daniel died, God lost His intercessor, and the whole political scene swung around to serve satan rather than God. Cambyses II went against the edict of his own father and stopped the building of the temple for over seven years. Then another pretender to the Persian throne, Artaxerxes I, continued to prevent the building for yet another seven years.

These kings actually violated the law and the constitution of the Persian-Median Empire in order to do this and have their own despotic way. All of God's people lost heart, and even their apostolic leader, Zerubbabel, diverted his attention to other things.

So 14 years went by with everything at a standstill. Then, two young prophets named Haggai and Zechariah gained their spiritual vision. With the same spirit of prayer as Daniel, they started to prophesy and pray and rouse others to pray. Haggai in particular prophesied to the immediate situation and stirred the disillusioned builders to action. Infused with a new spirit, they were empowered to get back to building again. These two prophets also began to pray change into the political situation. Then the evil king was suddenly killed and replaced by another son of Cyrus called Darius II.

Darius II was a mild and reasonable man. When the facts were reported to him of what his father had decreed concerning the rebuilding of the temple, he said, "What are we doing? We should have never stopped the Jews from building the temple again. First of all, it's against the law and the constitution of the Persia-Media Empire; second, it will also bring the wrath of their God upon us. Give them the finances they need from government funds and do everything you can to help them get this job finished." (See Ezra 6.)

This prompted a major change in the political climate, as well as in the spirit of God's people. It all happened because God found two new prophetic intercessors to replace Daniel. The Spirit of the Lord came upon these dispirited Jews, and in four years they completed what they had been saying was impossible to do for the preceding 14 years. The temple was dedicated in 515 B.C.

Can you see this very crucial and vital role of intercession? It does not require many people. One or two are enough. They can be as seemingly insignificant and lacking in natural influence as that little widow-woman, but if they know how to pray, they can elect a new president and decide who is going to rule over the nation.

Once you know how to rule in your prayers, you can choose the mayor of your town, the federal and state judges of your state or city, your political representatives, the chief of police, and so forth. There is power in intercession. We need intercessors who can clearly hear God and then, through their prayers and the right God-directed activism, get into the realms of politics, the judiciary, law enforcement, education, and the media so His Kingdom can truly come.

The kingdom of satan has long been established on Earth and is still here until the Kingdom of God comes to forcibly replace it. There is no vacant, neutral territory anywhere in the world. Therefore, every attempt to establish the Kingdom of God is automatically an invasion of what satan has illegally occupied and now regards as his territory. That is why the Kingdom of God always suffers violence and is vigorously attacked the moment it appears to be gaining ground. The only way to deal with that demonic violence is to be even more spiritually violent in our response.

Satan understands the strategic role of cities, and he set up his spiritual power centers long ago establishing his rule from there. Satan knows that whoever controls the cities will also control the surrounding territories. Throughout the world, almost without exception, the cities of the nations are the strongholds of satan's kingdom, and they must be taken before the Kingdom of God can really come. Therefore, we must learn the tactical principles of spiritual warfare in order to be effective warriors in the Lord's Army in the critical days ahead.

It is exciting to know we won't be fighting alone, as we are about to learn in the next chapter.

ENDNOTES

1. Alan Vincent, *Heaven on Earth: Releasing the Power of the Kingdom through YOU* (Shippensburg, PA: Destiny Image Publishers, 2008).

2. Information on the Argentinean Revival and Omar Cabrera's involvement in it is available on several different websites. See Peter Wagner, "The Awesome Argentina Revival—Lessons in Evangelism"; www.openheaven.com/library/history/argentina.htm; accessed August 1, 2011; and *Vision of the Future,* http://www.visiondefuturo. org/found.html; accessed August 1, 2011.

CHAPTER 2

A BALANCED UNDERSTANDING
OF ANGELS AND DEMONS

MANY references to angelic and demonic activity are found in both the Old and New Testament. According to the PC Study Bible Concordance, the subject of demons is referred to 74 times in the Bible, four times in the Old Testament and 70 times in the New Testament. Angels are mentioned nearly 300 times in the whole Bible, with over 100 references in the Old Testament and nearly 200 in the New Testament. Messenger angels are particularly active in supporting and communicating with human prophets and prayer-warriors, such as Daniel, as they waged war against demonic principalities and powers in the Old Testament.

I remember very well one incident in my own ministry, which occurred some years ago when I was in Hyderabad, India, for a leaders' conference. God had shown me that I was to address the issue of the widespread poverty in the region, but I had told no one that this was my subject.

When I arrived, there was great excitement because a very large angel— over 60-feet tall—had appeared in the church compound a few days before and was seen by a group of leaders. The angel spoke and said, "My name is 'Prosperity' and I have come to destroy the spirit of poverty in this region." It then stretched out its hands toward the building in which we were to meet and flashes of lightning went from its fingers and struck the building. As I prayed over this, God said to me that it was a sign to confirm the message I was bringing. He then told me that when an angel comes in the size and appearance of a man, it has come as a messenger angel; but when it comes in this massive size, it has come as a warring angel.

We had an amazing time in that conference, and I was given authority by Jesus to pray and break the curse of poverty. Within five years of that incident, the economy of many of the believers and the economy of the overall region had changed significantly for the better.

I could tell a number of similar stories in my own experience in India, Africa, and even in America, where angels have appeared and encouraged us to pray and sometimes commanded me to speak a very specific word of authority against a dangerous demonic attack. In every case, it caused a dramatic change for the better to take place.

Our Bibles record that angels were deeply involved in the preparation and protection of Elizabeth, the mother of John the Baptist. We also read that Zacharias, the father-to-be, was sternly rebuked by the angel Gabriel when he doubted the message which the angel had brought straight from the presence of God concerning her miraculous conception. As a punishment, Zacharias remained dumb until the baby was born (see Luke 1:11-20).

There was much angelic participation with Mary and Joseph in the preparation for the birth and protection of the Baby Jesus after His birth. Massive choirs of thousands of angels were seen by the shepherds in the fields around Bethlehem celebrating the birth of the Savior.

There are almost 50 references in the three synoptic Gospels alone describing the angelic activity directly involved with the birth, ministry, suffering, death, and resurrection of the long-awaited Messiah. Several powerful Old Testament prophecies warn us of greatly increased activity by mighty angels at the end of the age.

We need to be prepared and ready to work effectively with them. If we are going to be at all effective in spiritual warfare, we must seek God to teach us and give us a working knowledge of these spiritual beings. Only then are we going to succeed to any degree against demonic powers and be able to forcefully advance the Kingdom of God.

As we begin to recognize the reality of the spirit realm and become more sensitive and responsive to angels and more aware of the demonic, we will need to recognize that compared with Christians from Africa and Asia, most Christians who have grown up and lived in our Western society are very immature and undeveloped regarding the exercise of their spirit person. People from these other continents are often much more aware and sensitive to the spirit realm because they have been frequently exposed to powerful manifestations of demonic spirit powers in their cultures.

But when these brothers and sisters are truly and powerfully converted and delivered from every demon, this knowledge of the spirit realm can then work to their advantage. When they are then filled with the love and presence of the Father and the risen Christ and then baptized with the presence and power of the Holy Spirit, they can quickly become mighty spiritual warriors who know how to wage effective warfare against the demonic powers that formerly enslaved them.

Generally, in our Western culture, we have done an excellent job of developing the physical and intellectual parts of our humanity, but often the spirit person has remained an immature babe.

I personally am grateful that I went to India as a fairly new Christian after a life-transforming encounter with Jesus Christ. I was spiritually less than five years old when I first arrived. So I grew up spiritually in India, where I was soon thrown into open and obvious conflict with strong demons.

Through the sheer necessity of survival, Eileen and I quickly learned to fight and overcome these demons in Jesus' mighty name. So I am not typically Western in my outlook in these matters, and I thank God for that.

When we look at what the New Testament has to say about demons and angels, we find their activity in the battle of the two kingdoms is recognized as an important factor in the war. Through Jesus and the apostles (Paul and John particularly), we are urged to wrestle and fight against this spiritual wickedness in heavenly places (see Eph. 6:12; 1 John 4:1-4).

We are also warned, particularly by Jesus and the same two apostles, not to allow ourselves to be deceived by the many demonic counterfeits which will especially appear in the last days, such as demons masquerading as angels of light (see 2 Cor. 11:14). We are also warned in Scripture to beware of false prophets and false prophecies, false apostles, false claims of angelic visitations, false angelic visions, and strange suspect revelations. We are specifically told to reject them (see 1 John 4:1-6; 2 Cor. 11:1-13).

Yet at the same time, we are told not to despise all these things, but to test everything by the biblically prescribed tests and hold fast to that which is good.

In Matthew 7:15-20, Jesus taught that we would know the good and the false prophets by the fruit of their lives. He said in verse 18: *"A good tree cannot bear bad fruit, nor can a bad tree bear good fruit."*

John's epistles carefully teach us that we must test the spirits of those who claim to be His ministers to see if Jesus has really been manifested in their flesh. Their lifestyles need to exhibit the character, humility, gentleness, and righteousness of Jesus before we can trust what they say or do (see 1 John 3:24—4:6).

In a long passage from Second Corinthians 10:12 right through to Second Corinthians 11:15, Paul listed the unpleasant characteristics of false apostles and those who exalt themselves and compare themselves with others and also seek to extract money from people. He told the saints in Corinth that the activities of such people come from another Jesus, another Gospel, and another spirit (see 2 Cor. 11:4) which is false, and they should have nothing to do with them. Moving in a right balance of these things will greatly assist us to see many victories in the war ahead.

When I began to research this topic, I was surprised to discover that very little had been written on the subject of angels in the past 30 years, but recently things have begun to change. The subject of angels and demons has become prevalent in books and movies, yet we must use great discernment in what we read and view. Satan is using the media to infiltrate the minds and hearts of our children and adults as well, enticing them to dabble in ungodly practices with demonic games. Witchcraft is blatantly presented in books and movies like *Harry Potter,* and now vampires are taking center stage.

The war between the kingdom of darkness and the Kingdom of God is intensifying, and we need to learn how to use the weapons God has provided for us.

CHAPTER 3

A GREAT WEAPON OF
OUR WARFARE

JESUS began His Kingdom ministry with a mighty flow of healings and miracles accompanied by the casting out of many demons. As soon as He was anointed and returned from the wilderness having won His battle with the devil, He began to preach the Kingdom of God with healings and miracles. Multitudes followed Him wherever He traveled (see Matt. 4:23-25).

Moving in the miraculous is one of the mightiest weapons in our armory against the devil's evil accusations and deceptive lies. One miracle can convince thousands of skeptics. Several times, in various ways, Jesus said to the hostile scribes and Pharisees: "If you can't believe Me for My words, then believe Me for my works. My works testify of Me" (see John 5:33-36, 10:37-38, 14:10-11).

As soon as Jesus received the news that John the Baptist had been imprisoned, He made preparation for an even more powerful expansion of the Kingdom. Jesus' immediate response was to intensify the flow of the supernatural. This was Jesus' way of responding to the attacks of the devil. He would go against satan and counterattack even more strongly with mighty signs, wonders, and miracles.

After that initial breakthrough of the miraculous, He sat down and taught the multitude the essential elements of the Kingdom of Heaven in His great discourse called the Sermon on the Mount. We find this great teaching most fully recorded in Matthew's Gospel, from the beginning of chapter 5 through the end of chapter 7. When Jesus had finished speaking, the miracles flowed even more powerfully. We read of many of these in Matthew chapters 8 and 9 and right on to the end of this great Gospel.

Although Jesus healed all their sicknesses and cast out all their demons, He knew the people needed much more than just physical healing. They were still harassed and helpless, like sheep without a shepherd. Laborers were needed who could gather them into the Kingdom of God and then patiently teach them and train them how to live victoriously in the power of the Kingdom. To truly save and protect them from the devil, they had to be brought under His Lordship and submitted to His loving, shepherding care through those He delegated and empowered to lead them. These shepherds were to patiently teach and train them to make them into His disciples.

Jesus then chose His 12 disciples, gave them further instructions, and sent them out as apostles. At this point, they were to go only to the lost sheep of the house of Israel and preach the Kingdom of Heaven. In addition to preaching, He gave them power and authority and commanded them to heal the sick, raise the dead, and cast out demons just as He had been doing (see Matt. 9:35-10:8; Luke 9:1-5).

He then commissioned another 70 of His disciples. This time they were not sent just to the Jews, but they were to go out two-by-two in His name into all the cities and surrounding nations where He Himself would come. Again He sent them out to heal the sick, cast out demons, raise the dead, and proclaim that the Kingdom of God had come (see Luke 10:1-11).

The 70 disciples came back with great joy because even the demons were subject to them through His name (see Luke 10:17). Jesus responded, saying, *"I saw Satan fall like lightning from heaven"*(Luke 10:18). He rejoiced in the Spirit and thanked the Father for hiding these things from the clever and the intelligent and revealing them to babes (see Luke 10:18-21). This is the only place in the Gospels where we find Jesus rejoicing in the context of His disciples moving out into the devil's territory in the power of supernatural signs and wonders to establish His Kingdom and reap a great harvest.

When Jesus was with His disciples in the upper room at the Last Supper, the major thing He taught them was that after His ascension, once the Spirit had come, He would show them the Father (see John 16:12-15). Then they would be able to become rightly related to the Father and would know the same intimacy with the Father that Jesus had always enjoyed.

Then the Father, the Spirit, and the risen Jesus would all come and dwell within them (see John 14:16-23). Their bodies would become the actual dwelling place of God. All three Persons of the Godhead would come and live within them in exactly the same way that the Spirit and the Father had dwelt within the humanity of Jesus during His days on earth. The same awesome relationship is available to us, and we should embrace and reverence it wholeheartedly.

Jesus also taught them that as long as they loved Him and obeyed Him in the same way that He had loved and obeyed the Father, they would do the same works that He had been doing and would go on to do even greater works in the much greater power of His resurrection (see John 14:12,17,23, 15:10).

These mighty miracles and healings were the powerful cutting edge of every evangelistic breakthrough in the days of the early Church and the means of establishing every church in the New Testament. It has continued the same way throughout church history and is still the same today.

DEFINING MIRACLES AND HEALINGS

Let's first be clear about what certain words used in the New Testament really mean. The main ones are as follows:

👑 *Miracles*—They were often called "signs." The word in the Greek is *semeion,* which refers to an attesting work or sign.[1]

☫ *Wonders*—The word denotes an act of wonder. The original Greek word is *teras*—which refers to an omen, a supernatural wonder, or "portent."[2]

In the cases where these words were used, the normal physical laws of the universe were visibly overruled by the power of God. As a result, the people were filled with awe and wonder.

In recounting healings, the New Testament uses three Greek words interchangeably, even when the same incidents are cited in the different Gospels.

☫ *Iaomai*— "To be cured, to be healed" (see Matt. 8:13; Luke 5:17).[3]

☫ *Therapeuo*—"To be cured, especially through adoration and worship"

☫ *Sozo*—This is the most frequently used word. It is found in all four Gospels and is used in the following three ways: "to be made whole physically; to be saved from our sins; to be delivered from demon-possession."[4] In other words, it means to be released from every work of satan. This particular word was used interchangeably in all three senses. Faith was always the agent by which these things occurred.

MIRACLES AND SIGNS ARE UNLIMITED

There were many events in the Gospels, the Book of Acts, and the Old Testament by which God overruled the normal physical laws of the universe and did some mighty attesting signs.

Many such miracles occurred through Moses, Joshua, Elijah, Elisha, and others—as well as Jesus and the apostles and some other disciples.

The first miracle Jesus did was to turn water into wine at the wedding in Cana (see John 2:3-11).

Several times Jesus rebuked storms on the Sea of Galilee in exactly the same way that He rebuked demons in people. There was always immediate calm as the violent winds and waves instantly ceased (see Matt. 8:23-27; Mark 4:35-41; Luke 8:22-35).

Jesus miraculously multiplied the five loaves and two fishes and fed 5,000 men plus women and children (a crowd of at least 20,000) with large amounts of food left over. On a separate occasion, He performed a similar miracle when He fed the 4,000. (See Mark 6:35-44, 8:1-9.)

On Jesus' instructions, Peter caught a fish with a coin in its mouth and used it to pay their temple taxes (see Matt. 17:27).

Jesus miraculously walked on the water of the Sea of Galilee in the midst of a great storm, and Peter temporarily followed Him until he doubted (see Matt. 14:25-32).

Jesus caused two miraculous draughts of fish to be caught by the disciples (see Luke 5:4-11; John 21:1-6).

Philip was supernaturally transported after speaking to the eunuch (see Acts 8:38-40).

Paul was unaffected by a poisonous snake that bit him after they were shipwrecked and washed ashore on the island of Malta (see Acts 28:1-6).

DISTINGUISHING HEALINGS FROM MIRACLES

A Healing

A healing has taken place when the demonic activity causing the sickness in a person's body is brought to an end. Although the demonic attack may be instantly terminated, the physical recovery may take place slowly and naturally afterward.

In some cases, the physical damage already caused by the disease may remain, but any further ravaging of the disease is immediately and permanently stopped.

A Miracle

A miracle has occurred when the healing includes a creative or restorative act of divine power that repairs or replaces damaged or missing parts of the body. Some Biblical examples are described below.

The Healing of the Blind Man

In John 9:1-7 we read that with this particular blind man, Jesus made clay by taking dirt from the ground and mixing it with His spittle. He then laid it on the blind man's eyes and told him to go and wash in the Pool of Siloam, which means "sent" or the Sent One.

The man followed Jesus' instructions and came back seeing. I believe Jesus healed him in this particular way using the dust of the ground mixed with His spittle (symbolic of His Word) so as to be an allegorical picture to remind us of how man was created from the dust of the ground by the Word of God. This suggests to me that the blind man possibly had empty eye sockets and had new eyes created for him out of nothing (although I'm not being dogmatic about this).

I experienced this personally about 25 years ago in India. A man came forward after I had preached at a meeting in Chennai (or Madras as it was then called). He came to be healed, and when he stood in front of me, I saw that he had one empty eye socket.

I asked him what he wanted God to do for him. He pointed to his empty eye socket and indicated that he wanted a new eye. I was a bit taken aback, but I laid my hand on this empty eye socket and prayed. I have to admit that I did not pray with very much faith. When I took my hand away a few moments later, I was totally shocked to see a brand new eye blinking at me from this formerly empty eye socket. It was a glorious miracle. After many years, I was recently back in Chennai, and this same man came forward, greeted me, and reminded me of the amazing miracle God had done for him that day.

Scripture records a number of such creative miracles that Jesus did, including the following:

1. A man with a withered arm was healed in the synagogue on the Sabbath. His arm was stretched out and fully restored to normal function again (see Luke 6:6-10).

2. A woman who was doubled over was instantly straightened (see Luke 13:10-13).

3. The lame man at the pool of Bethesda was raised up and walked after being paralyzed for 38 years (see John 5:1-9).

4. Peter raised the lame man at the Gate Beautiful (see Acts 3:1-10).

5. Paul was raised up after being stoned and left for dead at Lystra. He had no residual injuries, because they disappeared immediately (see Acts 14:19-20).

6. On several occasions Paul's apostolic ministry was confirmed to skeptics by the signs, wonders, and mighty deeds which God did through him (see 2 Cor. 12:11-12).

Lazarus Raised From the Dead

Lazarus was raised from the dead four days after he had died, and his body was already decomposing. Jesus deliberately waited those four days so as to make this particular miracle a sign of His authority over death and to show that He already was the Resurrection and the Life. Therefore, those who believed in Him would not die permanently, even if they died physically.

When Jesus came to the tomb of Lazarus, He had already prayed and already obtained the answer from His Father. So when He came to the tomb, He did not pray for Lazarus again. He just thanked the Father that He had already heard Him and commanded Lazarus with a loud voice to, "Come forth!" Lazarus immediately came forth. Those watching the miracle released him from his grave clothes and joyfully believed. The story immediately spread like wildfire to many nations (see John 11:1-44).

SICKNESS, DISEASE, AND DEMONIC ACTIVITY

Sickness and disease are linked to demonic activity. In Acts 10:38 Peter summarizes the ministry of Jesus as follows:

> *God anointed Jesus of Nazareth with the Holy Spirit and with power, who went about doing good and healing all who were oppressed by the devil...*

There are many more such examples in Scripture (see Matt. 10:1, 8; Mark 1:32-34; Luke 6:17-19, 9:1-2). Jesus rebuked sicknesses in the same way that He spoke to those who were obviously demon-possessed. We have already seen that Jesus rebuked violent demonic storms on the Sea of Galilee in exactly the same way, using exactly the same words. When He spoke, the storms immediately ceased, and the sea became calm.

Demons may be resident within people and may need casting out for the healing to take place; or the demons may be afflicting or attacking from the outside and need to be thrown off. They can reside in particular families and be passed down from generation to generation. They can be the result of witchcraft curses put upon people, or the people themselves could have been directly involved in witchcraft or one of the false cults, particularly Freemasonry. In every case, the demonic spirit has to be rebuked and cast out.

Certain high-ranking demons are more stubborn and require a greater authority and faith to cast them out. This authority and faith only comes through a life of prayer and fasting (see Matt. 17:14-21; Mark 9:17-29).

The bottom line influencing everything else is an effective prayer life. Jesus demonstrated this and also taught it continually to His disciples. But always, it must be a prayer of faith. Just praying for people is not enough. It is only the prayer of faith that heals the sick (see James 5:14-15). It must be more than a prayer of sympathy or of pleading desperation or of mere hoping that God will do something to get results. It takes more than looking to Jesus and seeing Him as one of several different options to be tried. Faith rests in *believing* in Jesus and the power of His Word.

The only biblical reason ever given by Jesus for failure to see anyone healed or delivered was always unbelief. The only reason that Jesus ever gave for failure to do miracles like Him in His name was unbelief. He never rebuked His disciples for stepping out and trying to copy Him and do His works; nor was it considered by Him as presumption. He certainly never told them it was not God's will to heal anybody or to stop praying.

Not only can unbelief prevent us from receiving deliverance or healing, but it can also prevent us from ministering healing or deliverance effectively to others. The failure of the father to see his demonized son healed was identified by Jesus as unbelief. Jesus also said that the failure of the disciples to heal the same demonized boy was because of their unbelief (see Mark 9:17-29).

THE DEFINITION AND SOURCE OF REAL FAITH

This subject is fully covered in my earlier book *The Good Fight of Faith,*[5] which I strongly recommend should be read and fully absorbed if you wish to be effective in spiritual warfare and move in the miraculous. In the meantime, I will share some key points from that book.

I recommend meditating on Paul's fourfold exhortation to Timothy in First Timothy 6:12-14. This was written as Paul came to the end of his personal race of faith and was handing the baton over to Timothy to continue the race:

1. Fight the good fight of faith.

2. Lay hold of the eternal life to which he was called.

3. Maintain a good confession before many witnesses.

4. Remember the good confession of Jesus before Pontius Pilate.

I would also note a few more important keys to walking in faith:

⚜ Without faith it is impossible to please God (see Heb. 11:6).

⚜ We must run the race of faith with perseverance (see Heb. 12:1-2).

⚜ We must have a sober, honest assessment of the measure of faith that Christ has dealt us (see Rom. 12:3).

The best Bible definition of faith is found in Hebrews 11:1: *"Faith is the assurance of things hoped for, the conviction of things not seen"* (NASB). The Greek word translated "assurance" (or "substance" in the New King James Version) is *hupostasis,* which refers to a "title deed."[6] This genuine, legal title deed is sufficient proof that the things for which we have faith are already there in the heavenly realm, but are not yet manifested in the physical world in which we live.

As Hebrews 11:1 reveals, faith is also the convincing proof (translated "conviction" in the New American Standard Bible and "evidence" in the New King James Version). The Greek word here is *elegchos.*[7]

Faith cannot create; it can only obtain. The only vehicle that can create things out of nothing is the Word of God. When God speaks, out of His being comes forth a creative force that is called His Word. God calls things which *are not* into existence; He creates them out of nothing, and *they are!* In that way, what He speaks come to life in the realm of the spirit and remains there eternally alive just waiting for faith to get hold of it. In other words, it has the power to bring you from dreams to substance, from hope to faith.

Faith comes by hearing the specific spoken Word of Christ (see Rom. 10:17). It is not enough to just read His promises or even memorize them. We must truly hear God speak these words in our spirits, then receive them, truly knowing that what He has said has become part of us. Once we have grasped the full weight of what He has already declared, we can then be fully confident that what He has said will come to pass—in spite of circumstances or whatever we see with our natural senses.

It's not what we imagine or desire naturally, but only what we have heard God say in our spirits that is the foundation for true faith.

TRUE FAITH—A GIFT FROM GOD

We cannot create real faith from within ourselves. We can only gratefully receive this ability to truly believe as a gift that comes to us from God.

Mark 11:22-24 is a key passage in understanding how faith works. What Jesus literally said in this important verse can be explained in my expanded paraphrase as follows: "Peter, you must have, or learn to receive, or actively take hold of, the gift of God's faith or God's own ability to believe. Then you can speak a word of real faith and it will happen."

Faith is an intrinsic part of God's eternal life. Only God knows how to believe. He simply cannot doubt; that's impossible with God. A true believer must be continually filled with His eternal life and not live out of his or her own soul life. Our natural soul life or "flesh" cannot believe; it can only doubt.

In our spirits, we can step into the spirit realm by faith and take hold of what God has already spoken into eternal existence there. We can then firmly grasp this invisible unseen Word by faith, bring it out of the spirit realm, and cause it to manifest in this material time-space world so that it becomes physically visible for all to see.

The devil hates real faith because it has the power to destroy his kingdom. So he fights against it with all his might. God has already spoken and done everything necessary in the spirit realm to totally destroy satan and his kingdom.

When we bring God's Word to manifestation by our faith, it releases the power of God on Earth to destroy the devil and all his works.

That's why it's always a fight of faith. But in Scripture it's always a *good* fight of faith, because if we keep our faith, we will always win.

TRUE FAITH MUST BE TESTED

God has to allow our faith to be tested to prove that it is true faith. When we speak a word, even of real faith, there can sometimes be a delay while satan is allowed to argue his case and test whether our faith is genuine. If we persevere and do not stop believing, God will give the righteous judgment in our favor. As we have already seen, God also uses delay to train us to believe and develop our faith to make it even stronger for the next battle (see Luke 11:5-10, 18:1-8).

THE CRIPPLING POWER OF UNBELIEF

Unbelief is not just the absence of faith; it is much worse than that. Unbelief is a spirit from satan that will not let us believe even when it is reasonable to do so.

Faith and unbelief are two spirits that work the same way in the spirit realm. The first is from God, and the second is from satan. They both operate the same way on our human spirit and in the spirit realm to convince us of unseen things in spite of what we hear, see, or feel with our natural senses. With the faith of God we are still able to believe, in spite of any opposing factors we perceive with our natural senses.

Conversely, when unbelief grips us, we cannot even believe when our natural senses tell us we should. The scribes and Pharisees were gripped by this spirit of unbelief and refused to believe in Jesus, despite seeing many of His wonderful works. Their pride, sense of importance, and hunger for recognition and praise prevented them from coming to faith in Him (see John 5:44).

The 12 disciples were gripped with an amazingly strong spirit of unbelief concerning the resurrection of Jesus; they could not believe that He was risen, even when all the natural evidence said He was. They were paralyzed by unbelief until Jesus rebuked that spirit of unbelief and their hardness of heart. When that spirit was dealt with and cast out, they at last were able to believe (see Mark 16:12-20). He then commissioned His disciples to go and preach the Gospel of the Kingdom everywhere once they believed and were clothed with power (see Luke 24:46-49).

Unbelief is a spirit that takes hold of many people who have lived in a dead religious atmosphere. This spirit also affects those who have lived in a secular atmosphere where the natural mind and human intellect have become their "gods" for all practical purposes. Such people cannot believe anything they cannot rationally explain and intellectually understand. When we come to Christ from a traditional religious background or a rational, secular-humanistic background, that evil spirit is often already controlling us. We must come to hate it as God hates it and then call on God to deliver us from the power of that evil spirit and set out spirits free to receive the spirit of faith from God. Then our minds can be renewed, and we can begin to think like God, and as a result, we begin to believe like God.

This was certainly true in my case, and this inability to really believe continued to trouble me for years after I was truly converted and born-again. One wonderful morning as I was praying, God came to me and set me free. On that day, because of God's amazing grace, I received the gift of faith and began to think like God (See Rom. 12:2).

ENDNOTES

1.   *Blue Letter Bible,* "Dictionary and Word Search for *miracle* in the NKJV," 1996-2011, http:// www.blueletterbible.org/search/ translationResults.cfm?Criteria=miracle&t=NKJV (accessed June 7, 2011).

2. *Blue Letter Bible,* "Dictionary and Word Search for *teras* (Strong's 5059)," 1996-2011, http:// www.blueletterbible.org/lang/lexicon/ lexicon.cfm?Strongs=G5059&t=KJV (accessed June 7, 2011).

3. See *Strong's Exhaustive Concordance*, Greek # 2390, and *Young's Analytical Concordance* for many examples.

4. *Biblesoft's New Exhaustive Strong's Numbers and Concordance with Expanded Greek-Hebrew Dictionary.* CD-ROM. Biblesoft, Inc. and International Bible Translators, Inc. (© 1994, 2003, 2006) s.v. "Sozo," (NT 4982).

5. Alan Vincent, *The Good Fight of Faith* (Shippensburg, PA: Destiny Image Publishers, 2008).

6. W.E. Vine, *Vine's Expository Dictionary of New Testament Words,* Blue Letter Bible (1940, 1996), s.v. "Assurance, Assure, Assuredly," <http://www.blueletterbible.org/Search/Dictionary/viewTopic.cf m?type=GetTopic&Topic=Assurance,+Assure,+Assuredly&DictList =9#Vine's> (accessed June 7, 2011).

7. *Biblesoft's New Exhaustive Strong's Numbers and Concordance*, s.v. "Elegchos," (NT 1650).

CHAPTER 4

EXPERIENCING
A FLOW OF MIRACLES

M ANY things impact the flow of miracles, but here we are going to focus on three main factors that influence our ability to experience their wonder.

THE FIRST FACTOR—HAVING THE RIGHT ATMOSPHERE

The right atmosphere is produced by the constant believing prayer of a community of God's people amongst whom the power of the Lord is present to heal. During Jesus' earthly ministry, He had to do this all by Himself, and He longed to have others join Him in prayer who would pray with such power. We find Jesus frequently going apart to pray by Himself, often all night. As a result, the power of the Lord was present to heal (see Mark 6:46-56; Luke 6:12-19).

Once the Spirit had come, after the ascension of Jesus, the disciples were empowered to pray, and a flow of miracles immediately began as they burst out of the upper room on the Day of Pentecost. Faith and expectancy were generated by the way this community prayed. All unbelief and contrary spirits were chased away and great boldness came upon the disciples. The signs and miracles were more often done through the hands of the apostles, but anybody who believed could be used, such as Stephen and Philip.

We sometimes see today that healings and miracles happen spontaneously during a time of prayer and worship because the atmosphere is so powerful. It is the corporate faith and prayer of a whole body of believers and the increasing presence of the Lord which produce an atmosphere that causes these things to happen (see Luke 5:16-17; Acts 4:24-33).

On the other hand, if chronic unbelief rules the atmosphere as it did in the synagogue in Jesus' hometown of Nazareth, nothing can happen. The atmosphere was so badly polluted that even Jesus could do no miracles there, and He marveled at their unbelief (see Mark 6:5-6).

Part of their problem was that they had known Jesus for many years before He was anointed with power. They were very familiar with "Jesus the carpenter" who made furniture and who sometimes read the set Scriptures in the synagogue at the weekly Sabbath meeting. But they refused to receive this Jesus, who had come back from the wilderness anointed with power, because He was a total stranger to them. So they angrily rejected Him and even tried to kill Him.

Many nominal Christians make the same mistake. They have been going to the same traditional church for decades and have never seen a miracle or supernatural healing. They are very familiar with the gentle, meek, and mild Jesus they have grown up with in Bible stories, but the Jesus of power is a total stranger to them. When this Jesus suddenly shows up as He did in Nazareth, they sometimes respond in the same way and cry out, "This is of the devil!" and chase Him out of the church (see Mark 6:1-6; Luke 4:16-30).

When Jesus did a major miracle, like raising the dead, He always prevented the wailing, unbelieving mourners from entering the room with their despair and unbelief. This was done to keep the atmosphere clear of unbelief and full of expectant faith. This is graphically portrayed in the raising of Jairus' daughter, as seen in Luke 8:40-56.

Peter did the same thing when he entered the house of a woman named Tabitha (or Dorcas) who had already died in Joppa. When he arrived, he first put all the wailing women out of the room, then He knelt down and prayed. When he commanded Tabitha to arise, she did. (See Acts 9:36-42.)

We must learn to follow Jesus' and Peter's example and maintain the right atmosphere if we want to see these kinds of miracles. Do not allow negative, unbelieving people to sit in the front rows of any meeting when you desire to move in the miraculous. Fill those front rows with positive, believing intercessors so as to produce the right climate. This will make a big difference in how much God can do.

It must also be an atmosphere where no lying hypocrisy and chronic unbelief among God's people is allowed to remain (see Acts 5:1-16; Josh. 7:1-26).

I personally learned to do the same thing when I was privileged to work with the great evangelist Reinhard Bonnke in Africa many years ago. Getting the front rows full of faith-filled expectant people made a great difference to what happened in the meetings.

We also see this principle of first driving out evil and unclean spirits when Jesus drove out the money changers and religious thieves in the temple. The blind and the lame were able to come to Him there and be healed (see Matt. 21:12-14).

THE SECOND FACTOR—THE RIGHT VESSEL

For miracles and healings to flow, God needs an anointed person who has fulfilled the required conditions to be a holy "channel" of God's power. These conditions can be summarized as follows. (I'm using the pronoun *they* in this list, but obviously it includes all ages and both sexes):

1. They have developed and constantly maintain an effective personal prayer life with God the Father through the Spirit and the Son.

2. They live lives of intimate fellowship with the Father, the Son, and the Holy Spirit even while going about their ordinary daily affairs. They are constantly able to practice the presence of God and hear His voice.

3. They have actively dealt with and have cast away any residue of unbelief.

4. They have received real faith from God and have developed that faith by successfully passing through various God-ordained tests and trials to bring them to maturity.

5. They have received a definite impartation and/or anointing of power from God and are continually being filled with the Spirit and experiencing a daily inflow of the eternal life of God.

6. They live a genuine, holy, and separated life under the discipline of the Holy Spirit. This is not the same as being under a set of rules made by some legalistic so-called "holiness" movement; these tend to focus only on outward things concerning dress and aspects of behavior, rather than on matters of the heart. In the process of true sanctification, the Holy Spirit tailor-makes these disciplinary rules for us as individuals so as to gain some specific area of each of our lives. These individual disciplinary rules constantly change and move us on to fresh ground so that God can progressively bring the whole being—spirit, soul, and body—under His control. (See Matthew 5:21-48 for some examples of this.)

7. They are able to hear the voice of God and have sharpened that ability through a life of constant obedience to whatever God says.

8. They have learned to be like little children who just obey whatever God says, even when it doesn't necessarily make any sense to the natural mind at the time.

9. They are filled with the compassion of Jesus and a faith that works through love. They are deeply stirred by the needs of those around them and love to step out and be channels for God to meet those needs.

10. They are willing to pay the price and cost of carrying that anointing in terms of inconvenience, extra demands upon their time, opposition from the devil, and sometimes severe criticism from other Christians—without taking offense or failing to continue to love those who do such things.

11. They are not timid or afraid, but are willing to stir up and use the gifts imparted to them with God-given boldness, even in the face of opposition that might possibly threaten their lives.

12. They are willing to take their share in the sufferings for the Gospel according to the power of God (see 2 Tim. 1:6-8).

13. They are humble and teachable, willing to be corrected, and willing to learn from any mistakes.

14. They are eager to learn and be taught new things revealed by the Spirit of God and so remain on the cutting edge of whatever God is doing.

THE THIRD FACTOR—KNOWING HOW TO RECEIVE

Knowing how to receive from God is a key element of healings and miracles. It is necessary to properly prepare the people who are seeking healing. They must have faith within themselves; therefore, the barrier of unbelief must be removed. If people are passive, or even worse, if they are unbelieving, it is much harder for God to give them the healing which they are seeking.

They must also learn how to receive from God. There are many great biblical examples of those who knew how to receive, and they stand out against the general atmosphere of unbelief. Here are just a few to consider:

1) Luke 8:43-48—The Woman With the Issue of Blood

This woman had great conviction that Jesus was able to heal her and that her time was now. So she pushed through the crowd just to touch the hem of His garment, believing that it would be enough. As she touched His garment, her expectant faith sucked the healing power from Jesus like a spiritual vacuum cleaner. He felt the power go out from Him, and she was instantly healed.

Some years ago, I did a weekend seminar in Waco, Texas, on the subject of "Moving in the Miraculous." A woman came to the seminar with very advanced Parkinson's disease and attended every session. She was trembling all over and walking with great difficulty with the aid of a walker. At each session, she inched her way slowly to the front row and sat down, always in the same seat. She listened attentively to all that was taught. We finally came to the last teaching session at midday on Saturday, after which I had planned an afternoon break followed by an evening meeting of impartation and power, when we would move out in faith to see healings and miracles.

As I closed the final morning session and dismissed the class, this lady stood up in a very determined way and said, "I'm ready! Pray for me now!" I replied, "Let's wait until tonight; there will be a much better atmosphere." But she responded with a very determined, "No! My time is now!" She wouldn't move and was blocking my way out of the hall. So I reluctantly laid my hands on her and prayed for her. To my great surprise, the power of God hit her in a tremendous way. She was thrown to the ground and was totally healed. She got up, threw away her walker, and literally ran all around the hall. She had sucked that healing from Jesus through me in exactly the same way as the woman in Luke 8 had done, and I felt the power go through me.

2) Luke 7:1-9—The Roman Centurion With Great Faith

This Roman centurion was a remarkable man. He loved the Jewish nation and, even more amazingly, he loved his sick servant who was his slave. He sent some messengers to Jesus imploring Him to come and heal his servant. Then he changed his mind and sent another message to Jesus and said, "I'm not even worthy to have You come into my house, and I'm not worthy to come to You. Just speak the Word and my servant will be healed."

In verse 8, he gave the reason for his confidence. It could be paraphrased in the following way: "I also (just like You, Jesus) am a man under authority, so when I say to a soldier or a servant, 'Go and do this or do that,' they immediately go and do it. Their instant total obedience is motivated by their fear of Caesar, the Roman Emperor, under whose authority I live and by whom I speak. I, therefore, have great delegated authority over soldiers and servants, but not over demons, sicknesses, and diseases because the Caesar I serve has no authority over them.

"But I see that, in a way similar to me, You are also a Man under authority. But Your authority is so much greater than mine because the One You have placed Yourself under has much greater authority. He is almighty God, and He has all authority over all things, including the demon that is killing my servant. So, please, just speak the Word and my servant will immediately be healed."

Jesus marveled at the centurion's great faith; He spoke the Word and the servant was instantly healed.

3) Matthew 15:21-28—The Persistent Canaanite Woman

This woman got her demonized daughter healed by her persistent faith that simply would not take "No" for an answer. Jesus deliberately made it tough for her so as to develop her faith. But she passed every test and stepped over every obstacle that Jesus put in her way. He was finally able to say to her in verse 28: *"Woman, great is your faith! Let it be to you as you desire."* She went home, not only to a healed daughter, but with a developed warring faith that she would be able to use in many other situations.

BEING DESPERATE IS NOT ENOUGH

We also read of people who tried and failed to receive or minister healing successfully. In Mark 9:14-29, we read of the father of a demonized boy with epilepsy. This man was a hindrance to his son's healing because of his own unbelief. He was trying so hard to believe by his own efforts that he could not bring himself to the real faith, which only comes from God.

This man first tried to get his son healed by bringing him to Jesus' disciples. They prayed, but were not successful. Then when Jesus returned from the Mount of Transfiguration, the man cried out desperately to Jesus: *"...If You can do anything, have compassion on us and help us"* (Mark 9:22).

Jesus threw the responsibility straight back at the father and literally replied, *"If you can believe, all things are possible to him who believes"* (Mark 9:23). The man then cried out, *"Lord, I believe; help my unbelief!"* (Mark 9:24).

The unbelief of the disciples was also a significant factor. They had already tried to cast the spirit out, but found it impossible. Then Jesus Himself came on the scene. When Jesus, who was full of God's faith, rebuked the demon and commanded it to leave, it left immediately, and the boy was delivered.

These disciples had just returned from a successful mission trip on which they had been specifically sent by Jesus to heal the sick, cast out demons, and proclaim the coming of the Kingdom of God. They had already seen such things happening through them and were rejoicing that the demons were subject to them through His name. They were surprised and disappointed when they could not deliver this boy. So they asked Jesus, *"Why could we not cast it out?"* (Mark 9:28).

Jesus explained that in this particular case they were not just dealing with one of the ordinary rank-and-file demons that love to harass and torment people.

They were now being confronted with an evil spirit of greater order in the hierarchy of satan's kingdom. It was probably the ruling spirit of that region.

This spirit had decided to come against them because of their earlier success in casting out demons, and it was determined not to allow their earlier success in advancing the Kingdom of God to continue any further without a fight.

Jesus then explained to His disciples that to win at this level of spiritual warfare and to always be successful against this kind of spirit required a life of fasting and prayer that they did not yet have. As Jesus already lived that way and was already armed for this kind of warfare, He could deal with that kind of spirit instantly (see Mark 9:14-29).[1]

It is possible to see healings or miracles with only one of these three factors in place, but it is definitely harder to get the breakthrough, and the outcome is much more uncertain. However, when all three factors are working together, you will definitely see a continuous flow of healings and miracles.

MYSTERY OF ANOINTING AND IMPARTATION

Many examples can be found in the Old and New Testaments where the Spirit of God came upon people to empower them for some specific task. It required the anointing of the Holy Spirit and an impartation of the Spirit that was sometimes accompanied by the laying on of hands.

The Anointing of the Spirit: What is often called "the anointing" occurs when the empowering of the Spirit comes directly upon a person or a group of people in the atmosphere of God's presence and remains upon them either permanently or temporarily. There is no human agency involved.

One of the most significant incidences of this took place at the Jordan River when Jesus was baptized by John the Baptist. The Spirit of God descended upon Jesus in the form of a dove, and from that day He was anointed with the Holy Spirit and power, marking the beginning of Jesus' ministry on the earth (see Matt. 3; Mark 1; Luke 3; John 1).

Another equally significant incident occurred on the Day of Pentecost. The Spirit fell on all 120 people (including the apostles) in the upper room, and they were filled with the Spirit and all spoke in tongues (see Acts 2). Following that, numerous similar incidences of the Holy Spirit coming upon groups of people are recorded in the Book of Acts. Here are a few Scriptures of note:

In Acts 4, church members were praying after Peter and some of the apostles were arrested and thrown into prison. After being threatened, the apostles were released and warned not to speak anymore in the name of Jesus. However, they refused to obey that order. Instead, they went and joined the powerful prayer meeting that was already in progress. They called on God to give them great boldness and asked that God would confirm His Word by signs and wonders being done in the name of Jesus. The Spirit fell freshly upon them all, and their prayer was immediately answered with great signs and wonders and the reaping of a mighty harvest of souls.

In Acts 10:27-45, Peter preached at the house of Cornelius, and the Holy Spirit fell upon the Gentiles for the first time. Peter was not expecting this to happen; in fact, everybody was amazed that Gentiles had received the Spirit just as the Jewish believers had on the Day of Pentecost.

The Impartation of the Spirit: This is a transfer of power and gifting from one person to another by the laying on of hands as directed by the Lord. It is an effective act of impartation because they have been first instructed to do so by the Lord.

Some examples of the impartation of the Spirit are listed below:

1. *Peter laid hands on the first deacons.* They were chosen to minister to the poor. Two of them, Stephen and Philip, also received an impartation of the anointing that was upon Peter to heal the sick and do attesting miracles. They immediately launched out into a powerful ministry of signs and wonders that shook whole cities—Stephen in the city of Jerusalem and Philip in the city of Samaria (see Acts 6:2-8, 8:5-8).

2. *Peter and John went to Samaria.* After Philip had preached Christ and many people were baptized, Peter and John came to Samaria. As they laid hands on the many converts, the converts received the Holy Spirit (see Acts 8:14-18).

3. *Ananias came to Saul.* A few days after Saul's dramatic conversion on the road to Damascus, Ananias came to Saul and laid hands on him, in direct response to a powerful prophetic word from Jesus. Instantly, scales fell from Saul's eyes and he was healed of his blindness and filled with the Holy Spirit. He immediately went out to boldly preach Christ (see Acts 9:17-22).

4. *Paul went to Ephesus.* When Paul finally arrived there, he found a few disciples of John the Baptist praying. After spending some time with them in prayer, he asked the pertinent question: *"Did you receive the Holy Spirit when you believed?"* (Acts 19:2). But they only knew John's baptism unto repentance and knew nothing about the Holy Spirit. So he immediately laid his hands on them that they might receive the Holy Spirit; they then spoke with tongues and prophesied (see Acts 19:2-7).

5. *Paul laid hands on Timothy* (see 2 Tim. 1:6). *Also, the whole presbytery of elders in Ephesus laid hands on him* (see 1 Tim. 4:14). The actual gift that was imparted is not mentioned. However, Timothy was strongly cautioned by Paul not to neglect this gift through fear; Paul urged him to stir it up and take his share in the suffering that comes with moving in the power of God.

ACTIVATING YOUR GIFT BY FAITH

In all these cases, the anointing or impartation had to be activated by the people stepping out in faith to use the new ability imparted to them. It came from God, but was imparted through an obedient human agency.

Timothy was guilty through timidity and fear of not stirring up the gift that had been imparted to him. He needed to step out and put to work the anointing that he had already received. He had to continue to develop it by faith long after all the feeling and memory of the impartation experience had passed away (see 1 Tim. 4:14; 2 Tim. 1:6-8).

As we step out, we will make mistakes; but we will learn as we are tutored and corrected by the Holy Spirit. God's attitude is always to encourage us to take new Christlike steps of faith and, by exercising this faith, to make things happen that bring glory to the name of the Jesus we love and serve.

Needless to say, all this will be fiercely resisted by the devil who will try to prevent anybody from successfully moving into a ministry of signs, wonders, and miracles. We must persist to see a breakthrough.

Subsequent to my being baptized in the Holy Spirit, I have several times experienced a fresh anointing in my ministry. Some years ago, I had hands laid on me by someone already moving in the miraculous in a far greater measure than I had ever experienced. I'm not the sort of person who easily goes down "under the power" in a meeting. However, on this occasion, when hands were laid on me, the power of God really hit me; I lay on the floor for some time, unable to move.

During that time God spoke to me and said, "Alan, you don't know how much I hate the spirit of cancer and especially what it is doing to My people. I am anointing you tonight to become a sword in My hand to go and wage war against every manifestation of this foul spirit."

It was a great and wonderful experience at the time. But two or three days later, it was only a warm, wonderful memory, and all feelings had long since evaporated. Then I met my first person who was actually suffering from a severe, life-threatening attack of cancer. Without any special feelings, I decided to activate my new anointing by stepping out in faith and commanding this spirit to leave and this woman to be healed in Jesus' mighty name. As I stepped out and began to address this condition, I certainly felt a new authority and a new level of faith within me as I felt power go out from me.

A few days later I received the thrilling news that this lady was completely healed. Since then, I have received hundreds of such testimonies from people in many countries who have been totally healed from cancer by the power of Jesus working through me. I rejoice in the privilege of being used.

As a result of activating my gift, I have seen many wonderful miracles take place through my obedience. Nevertheless, I still have a lot to learn and am still pressing toward the goal set in Scripture by the apostle Paul in Philippians 3:10-14; it is the goal to fully know Him and see the full power of His resurrection flowing through me. Just like Paul, I'm still pressing on toward this high calling.

Most Christians I know who have eventually broken through into powerful healing ministries have testified that the anointing and power that they now carry didn't come to them without a tremendous fight of faith. They had to keep stepping out, sometimes for months or even years, before they saw any real success. It was only after a long, hard-fought battle of dogged faith that they finally saw the breakthrough. They then went on to gain a continuing and increasing victory over the opposing demonic forces.

A great historic example of this would be the story of Pastor Johann Christoph Blumhardt who was a Presbyterian pastor in Mottlingen in the Black Forest of Germany. I read his story as a young Christian many years ago, and it had a profound effect upon me. If you have never read his amazing story, I suggest you get a copy of his biography.[2]

Pastor Blumhardt lived from 1805 to 1880 and is recognized by many as being the man who restored the lost gift of healing back to the Church during a time of great apostasy in Europe. After tremendous battles were fought against the prevailing demonic forces, he saw an amazing breakthrough, which brought a powerful revival to his region with hundreds of amazing miracles and thousands of salvations. He paid a tremendous price to get there and had to persist for eight years before he saw the first miracle. But, after the initial breakthrough had come, the anointing just increasingly flowed.

LEARNING TO IMITATE JESUS

At the temple gate called Beautiful, Peter gave to the lame man what he said he had: It wasn't gold or silver, but it was the faith Peter had received from God. It enabled the man to stand and even leap to his own feet as he instantly responded and was healed (see Acts 3:1-10).

Let us also be like Peter, who exactly copied what he had seen Jesus do with Jairus' daughter (see Luke 8:49-56). When Peter came to Lydda and then to Joppa, he was used for a series of remarkable healings and miracles.

Peter said to Aeneas, *"Aeneas, Jesus the Christ heals you"* (Acts 9:34). Peter was aware that the healing was accomplished by the risen Lord Jesus Christ using Peter's humanity in the same way that the Father and the Spirit had earlier used the humanity of Jesus (see Acts 9:32-35). Just like Jesus, Peter put out the wailing mourners weeping over the body of Tabitha before he spoke to her. Then he said, "Tabitha, arise!" Immediately, she came back to life. (See Acts 9:36-42.)

Like Timothy, we must copy Paul, who copied Jesus. We can learn from other great examples in the Bible and in church history right up to this present day and "follow" or "imitate" them as they "followed" or "imitated" Christ. The Greek word used is either *mimetes*—which literally means "to mimic or exactly copy"[3] (see 1 Cor. 11:1; Eph. 5:1; 1 Thess. 1:6)—or the word *akaloutheo*—which can have the meaning "to step carefully and exactly in the footprints of someone who has gone before and is now showing you the way"[4] (see Matt. 4:22; Mark 1:20).

John said in his great first letter: *"He who says he abides in Him ought himself also to walk just as He walked"* (1 John 2:6).

In Colossians 2:6 Paul said: *"As you therefore have received Christ Jesus the Lord, so walk in Him."* This is, of course, done by faith.

Again in Romans 6:4 Paul said that *"...just as Christ was raised from the dead by the glory of the Father, even so we also should walk in newness of life."*

So, step out and start walking this way. Receive His anointing and activate your spiritual gifts; you'll be amazed at what God will do through you to the glory of the name of Jesus and for the blessing of many.

ENDNOTES

1. This topic is dealt with much more fully in my book *The Good Fight of Faith*: (Shippensburg, PA: Destiny Image Publishers, 2008).

2. A recently published version of Pastor Blumhardt's biography is available: Friedrich Zundel, *Pastor Johann Christoph Blumhardt: An Account of His Life* (Eugene, OR: Wipf and Stock Publishers, 2010).

3. *Strong's Exhaustive Concordance*, Greek #3401, 3402.

4. *Strong's Exhaustive Concordance*, Greek #190.

CHAPTER 5

GOVERNMENT IN THE KINGDOM

FOR several centuries before Jesus came into the world, Europe, North Africa, and Western Asia were ruled by the Greek Empire, which was then followed by the Roman Empire. It was during this time that philosophy, the sciences, educational institutions, and libraries sprang up. Also, proper systems of government, backed by well-trained armies and the establishment of a government taxation system, were established all over these empires.

Even during the days of the Roman Empire, Athens remained the center of culture, philosophy, and education, with Greek philosophy and the Greek language dominating the intellectual life of these civilizations.

While Alexander the Great was still expanding the Greek Empire, he sent out military expeditions to conquer new territories and force the people to surrender to his rule. He then established governmental systems to consolidate his rule over them by appointing his officials in places of authority, thus making these people a loyal part of his empire.

During this time, the Greek words *apostello* meaning "to send out"[1] and *apostolos* meaning "a sent one" or "one sent forth…"[2] took on particular meaning.

When a military expedition was sent out by the emperor, the officer in charge was called an "apostle" and the military force under his command was called an "apostolate." The officer's task was to conquer the new territory in the name of the emperor, bring the people into willing submission to his rule, and then establish government and appoint loyal officials to continue to exercise authority in the emperor's name.

This was almost certainly in the mind of Jesus, the great Sent One of the Father, when He called the first 12 disciples "apostles" and sent them *(apostello)* to heal the sick, cast out devils, raise the dead, and proclaim that the Kingdom of God had come (see Matt. 10:1-8; Luke 9:1-2).

As I explained in my first volume on the Kingdom, titled *Heaven on Earth,* many chapters of the Old Testament are devoted to the subject of David's kingdom. This is not just for our information or to make us experts in Jewish history, but to give us precious insights into the Kingdom of God. These chapters contain the most complete and powerful allegories and pictures in all of Scripture of how the Kingdom of God is to be set up, ruled, and governed. They teach us how it is structured and how it functions, particularly on Earth.

David on his throne, and Solomon his son in his early years as king, provide powerful allegories and prophetic statements concerning the coming of Jesus as the King of His glorious Kingdom (see 2 Sam. 7:12-17; 1 Chron. 17:11-15).

Paul wrote in First Corinthians 10:1-11 that all these things in the Old Testament were written for our instruction, example, warning, and admonition. He said they were types and allegories of Christ and His Kingdom and they especially apply to those *"upon whom the ends of the ages have come"* (1 Cor. 10:11).

The very name *Kingdom of God* refers to the "rule"[3] or government of God. God's Kingdom only comes when He truly rules and His will is being done perfectly on Earth through His established government. We desperately need this to happen in every city and in every nation on earth. As Isaiah prophesied in Isaiah 9:6-7 concerning the coming of Jesus and His Kingdom, the first thing said about Him was that *"the government will be upon His shoulder";* concerning the Kingdom he said, *"of the increase of His government and peace there will be no end."* He concluded by saying that *"the zeal of the Lord of hosts"* would accomplish this.

In many parts of the world right now, there are local wars and conflicts with insoluble political and economic problems which are preventing any real peace, destroying economies, and diminishing the quality of people's lives. There can be no lasting peace or prosperity until His Kingdom fully comes.

DAVID'S STYLE OF LEADERSHIP

We can learn a lot about true Kingdom government from David's style of leadership and the government he established. Don't get the idea that David was an autocratic dictator. He certainly was not that. Nevertheless, he was a strong leader with a clear authority and a team of mighty men loyally serving him to establish his government and rule in every city.

He was God's appointed head and carried a final executive authority that every loyal leader recognized and submitted to. When David knew he had heard from God, he could say, "We will do this, and we will not do that." His subordinates then would agree and follow him. At the same time, however, he was personally meek and humble and very teachable so as to make sure he was really hearing from God.

A CLEAR, RECOGNIZED HEAD

This is always the true foundation of proper Kingdom government. It certainly does not depict a single autocratic dictator doing his own thing. Neither does it indicate a Kingdom run by a democratic committee or egalitarian board of elders or deacons who make every decision by consensus with various opinions being expressed and the final decision being rendered by a majority vote.

In Kingdom government there must always be a leader anointed and appointed by God who answers directly to Him. Such leaders must know their calling and be recognized by those who are in leadership together with them. This kind of leader seeks the wisdom and opinions of others, but has clear executive powers and a definite final authority.

We see the balance of this in First Chronicles 13:1, which says: *"Then David* **consulted** *with the captains of thousands and hundreds, and with every leader."*

David had already learned to hear from God as a shepherd boy in Bethlehem many years earlier. He knew that it had been God's will for him to become king over Israel and to establish a permanent dwelling place and worship center for God on Mount Zion in Jerusalem.

This lifelong passion of David is recorded in Psalm 132, which he wrote in his old age, after all his boyhood dreams founded upon these prophetic words had finally become reality. But even when David finally became king, he wanted from all his leaders an "Amen" to confirm what he knew God had already said to him many years before. He wanted it to become their vision as well as his.

Let's now read further in First Chronicles 13:2-3:

> *And David said to all the assembly of Israel, "If it seems good to you, and if it is of the LORD our God, let us send out to our brethren everywhere who are left in all the land of Israel, and with them to the priests and Levites who are in their cities and their common-lands, that they may gather together to us; and let us bring the ark of our God back to us, for we have not inquired at it since the days of Saul."*

CONSULTING SENIOR LEADERS FIRST

Notice the stages by which this decision was made. First, David had clearly heard from God. Second, he consulted with the most senior leaders who were themselves commanders of thousands. These were probably his mighty men described in Second Samuel 23:8-39 and First Chronicles12:1-40.

In the New Testament, these would be equivalent to the apostles, prophets, evangelists, pastors, and teachers of the Ephesians 4:11 ministries. These commanders of thousands agreed and said, "Amen, David! You're right on. We've heard the same thing from God." Then the prophets prophesied and said, "Amen,

David! We've just heard the same thing." Every one of these most senior leaders then agreed it was God's will.

"ENVISIONING" ALL THE LEADERS

When David went to the next level of leaders who were the captains of hundreds and fifties, it was the equivalent of what is described in the New Testament as the elders and leaders of local church congregations.

When David went to every other leader whose role was not precisely specified, it was allegorically representative of the final group that was comprised of all the other leaders with some area of responsibility in the churches. In our churches today, this would be representative of home group leaders and deacons plus any other people with leadership responsibility. The main purpose of going to every one of these lower level leaders was not so much to get their agreement or permission, but it was to "envision" them (or *impart* vision to them) so they would be gripped by the vision as strongly as David was. They would then embrace it actively as God's will and work with the same passion that David had. Because David took time to do this, they were also fully "envisioned" to see the tabernacle raised up on Mount Zion and the Ark brought back and placed inside it.

If you are the overall leader of a church congregation and you want the people you lead to catch your vision and run with it, learn these lessons from David. If your people are going to give themselves in zealous passion, they have to see the vision and own it as much as you do.

FINALLY, MOTIVATING ALL GOD'S PEOPLE

David would then go to all the people of Israel. David had heard from God concerning His will. Nevertheless, he knew the people of God couldn't jump enthusiastically into the purpose of God until they had seen it for themselves. He was not waiting for their permission to do it, but he was waiting for them to catch the same revelation he had, so they would be in faith with him concerning the vision. When they had seen it too, it became their vision as well as his. Then they would work zealously with him and give and sacrifice to make it happen.

If a leader comes to the people with an isolated, dictatorial attitude saying, "God has given me this vision, and I expect every one of you to be fully committed to it," he will not get the response he is looking for. He may have heard from God, but they have not. They cannot be in faith for something they have not seen or heard. If you give God the opportunity to bring your people to the same faith level as you, then you can lead them easily because they will be enthusiastic and faith-filled.

In John 10:1-18, Jesus said He was the Good Shepherd. He then carefully spelled out what that meant. He is the only door, and any legitimate minister has to come to the sheep through Him and be under His authority. Otherwise, they are thieves and robbers, even if they call themselves apostles or prophets.

Jesus made it clear that He loved His sheep and would lay down His life for them. He said, "My sheep hear My voice and they know Me and voluntarily follow Me" (see John 10:27).

In that sense, David was a true shepherd of God's people, so eventually all the people said to David, "Amen! We're with you!" It was then easy to lead them because they loved him, followed him, and now owned the same vision, as it says in First Chronicles 13:4: *"Then all the assembly said that they would do so, for the thing was right in the eyes of all the people."*

JAMES—HEAD OF THE JERUSALEM CHURCH

The New Testament equivalent to all this is seen in Acts 15. We are told quite clearly that James, the brother of Jesus, had the final headship authority of the Church in Jerusalem. Even though all of the remaining original 11 apostles were still resident in Jerusalem, it was necessary for a final executive head to be recognized over the home church. For some reason, which is not explained, the risen King Jesus chose James, who was His natural half-brother after the flesh. The Kingdom of God runs on headship; it doesn't run on committees, not even committees of apostles!

At that time, they had a difficult problem to solve, which was whether or not the converted Gentiles should keep the Law of Moses. When they came together to consider this matter, there were all kinds of conflicting opinions. Some were very sure of their doctrinal position. "The Gentiles have to be circumcised and keep the Law of Moses, otherwise they cannot be saved," they declared (see Acts 15:1). But Peter, Barnabas, and Paul now had a very different opinion because of their recent experiences with God, the Holy Spirit.

If you had heard the different opinions being so strongly expressed at the beginning of this first Council of Jerusalem, you would have thought there was no way they would be able to get unanimity over this issue. It looked more like they were going to end up with a church split. But look how the Spirit of God worked and used the leadership and wisdom of James: He went away and consulted with the apostles, who are the New Testament equivalent to the captains of thousands. Then they met with the elders, the New Testament equivalent to the captains of hundreds and fifties.

James listened to all the wisdom that was being poured out and to all the different opinions being expressed by various people, but most of all he was listening hard to God. The Spirit was saying to him, "That's good. Listen to what that person is saying; he's got it. Take note of that. But be careful here; that's not My wisdom, so just put it aside."

In all the mass of opinions being expressed, James got a clear strategy from the Spirit of God. Then God gave him supporting Scripture through the prophet Amos (see Acts 15:16-17).

After James had listened to the various opinions flying around the room, he gave the Church his judgment based upon the distilled wisdom of everything that they had heard. He didn't say, "The apostles have voted seven to five in favor." He didn't say, "The elders were forty-seven to three in favor." Instead, he said something like this: "Peter, Barnabas, and Paul have given their firsthand experience of the Spirit coming upon the Gentiles just as He did upon us at the beginning. I have weighed all the conflicting and different perspectives on this question. Now, I can see a clear strategy of God's wisdom through all of it. The Holy Spirit has also spoken to me and shown me that the Scripture in Amos 9:11-12 concerning the raising again of David's tabernacle is relevant here. If you look at all of this, you can see there is a clear answer from God; therefore, this is my judgment. I have used my apostolic wisdom to make a final appraisal; as a result, I am now telling you what we are going to do so that we can all be in agreement as one church body."

James then specified the necessary practicalities for the people of the Church, whether Jew or Gentile, to observe in order to allow this to happen. It tells us in Acts 15:22 that this judgment *"pleased the apostles and elders, with the whole church…."* Yes! The Holy Spirit was sitting in judgment saying through James, "This is My judgment, and this is the right decision."

They came from all those diverse positions to arrive at complete unity regarding what God was telling them to do. It says in Acts 15:30-31 that the decree sent from Jerusalem was enthusiastically received by the Church in Antioch. Are you getting a taste of how these things work?

From this Scripture we should learn that we are not to make decisions by the consensus vote of a committee. Neither should decisions be made by one autocratic leader imposing his will on the people. There is only one Lord of the Church, and His name is Jesus Christ! He is a gentle, loving, benevolent King and has perfect ability to command us through the Holy Spirit. Once He has spoken, we just need to get into line and do what He says. But in practice, it is difficult to ensure that His will is being flawlessly communicated. This is best done by means of a God-ordained protocol, which is carefully shown to us in Acts 15. The Kingdom of God cannot run effectively without that kind of government being in place. We need a proper procedure to ensure that we really know God's will.

RELEVANCE OF SCRIPTURE, THEN AND TODAY

To understand why Scripture was so relevant for the early Church and still is for us today, we need to go back to the early years of Solomon when David was still alive, but no longer king. We need to study both the manner in which the great temple of Solomon was built and the results of its being built.

Earlier in his reign, David was embarrassed to be living in such a splendid house while the Ark of the God of the whole earth was still in the original, simple tent that David had erected on Mount Zion at the beginning of his reign (see 2 Sam. 7:1-11). David longed to build a glorious temple worthy of the God he loved and served. So he began to make financial and material provision for a magnificent temple to be built by Solomon to house the Ark of the Covenant.

Nathan, the prophet, had initially encouraged David in his desire to build the temple because of the genuine devotion which was motivating David to do this. But he had spoken prematurely out of his well-meaning flesh. Later, when Nathan got alone with God and really heard His voice, God rebuked him and said it was not His will to do such a thing. So Nathan came back to David and corrected what he had said earlier on his own initiative.

Instead, he prophesied concerning the glorious spiritual building that David's greater Son, Jesus would one day build. It would be comprised of the "living stones" each believer would become through the power of the cross and the power of His resurrection. Now this spiritual building was a different matter and would gloriously become the dwelling place of God in the Spirit.

While God appreciated the sincere heart of David who wanted to do such a thing, He made it clear that, because He already filled the whole of Heaven and all the Earth, there was no building that could possibly contain Him; He would not allow people to confine His presence to some religious building, however glorious it might be in the eyes of humanity. God repeated the same message years later through the prophet Isaiah (see Isa. 66:1-5).

God knew the danger of splendid buildings becoming religious monuments that would actually become obstacles by taking people away from seeking and knowing God Himself. To know God personally and to be intimate with Him in Spirit through the mighty sanctifying power of the blood of the Lamb is far better and is the only true foundation of the New Covenant (see Heb. 8:6-13, 10:15-23).

However, God did allow Solomon to build the temple. I believe He allowed this for two reasons:

First, it became a powerful allegory of the true spiritual temple that Jesus, David's greater Son, would one day build out of the true living stones which His children would become.

Second, it showed what would happen to the hearts of the people when this outwardly glorious temple replaced both the tabernacle of Moses on Mount Gibeah and the simple tent which David had built on Mount Zion.

When the temple building was finally completed by Solomon, the tabernacle of Moses was taken down and raised up again inside this fabulous new building. The Ark of the Covenant was also removed from David's tabernacle and placed inside a curtained Holy of Holies inside the new temple. The curtains that had separated the three compartments of Moses' tabernacle were raised up inside the temple, and the Levitical priesthood was reestablished (see 2 Chron. 2-7).

The tabernacle of David was left standing on Mount Zion where it had been during the reign of David. But now it was abandoned and empty and no one came to it anymore. It finally fell down in ruins through sheer neglect, and no one even seemed to care.

As a result, the days of going directly into God's unveiled presence by the power of the blood of the New Covenant and in the liberty of the Melchizedek priesthood were over. No one entered directly into His presence anymore; the days of abandoned worship and the joyful face-to-face intimacy with God that was combined with holy reverence came to an end.

But, through the prophet Amos, God said that one day this tabernacle of David would be raised up again, fully restored, and its ruins repaired. As a result, a remnant of God's people would return to those days of worshipful, unveiled, face-to-face intimacy with God. There would again be a mighty outflow of power and miracles resulting in the rest of humankind seeking the Lord. This would bring in a mighty end-time harvest before the return of Jesus at the end of the age (see Amos 9:11-12; Acts 15:15-17).

SECURING THE CITY

For the full ruling power of a spiritual tabernacle of David to be experienced in a city, it must be a warring as well as a worshiping community. It must learn how to attack the demonic strongholds already established in the heavenly places and cast them down.

At the beginning of his reign, David built Jerusalem into a fortified city. One important principle of the Kingdom, which David vividly illustrates, is to give us understanding concerning the difference between cities and villages and their spiritual ability and power to exercise government over a region.

God gave David a strategy to establish his kingdom that has great meaning for all of us today. In the natural, to take over rulership of a country, a conquering king must always take control of the key cities. Occupying villages does not give a king rule over the land as long as the major cities remain untaken and continue to resist him. This is a fundamental principle of conquest. To rule the land, you must take the cities and subdue them.

India today is a classic spiritual example of what I am talking about. The whole democratic Republic of India is divided into about 30 states forming one federal republic. Each state is far more diverse and insular than the states of the United States of America. Each one is almost like a separate nation with its own language, culture, and customs. Nevertheless the whole of India is still one nation with one central federal government ruling over the whole of it.

Let us look at the State of Andhra Pradesh as an example. Andhra Pradesh means the "central province" and the capital city of the state is Hyderabad. This state, with a population of almost 80 million, is divided into about 350 regional subdivisions. Each of the subdivisions is called a "tarluk" and is similar to a county in the U.S. In each tarluk there is a main city called the tarluk headquarters city. Regional government offices are located in that city. From these offices, various government officials of city, state, and nation exercise rule over the whole tarluk.

Scattered around each tarluk are many small towns and hundreds of villages. The residents of these smaller communities come into this main city to buy and sell local produce, trade land, go to the bank, visit various government offices to get their government papers signed, and so forth. Everything important is done in these tarluk headquarters cities. They are like hubs from which everything is ruled and regulated for the whole of the tarluk.

Each of the hundreds of villages in a tarluk has a population ranging from a few hundred to maybe a few thousand. When God began to bring His Kingdom to this region, He told us not to spend our time primarily evangelizing the individual villages. Instead, He said we should go straight to the tarluk headquarters city and establish a regional church there.

From that regional center, we could then reach out to all the surrounding villages and smaller towns. These tarluk cities already were the centers of secular government and civil authority. God showed us that this natural administration was a pattern for bringing the Kingdom effectively to the whole region and a means of establishing proper spiritual rule. So we concentrated on first raising up a regional church in each tarluk city. From there we were to reach out to the surrounding villages and small towns. It has proven to be very successful.

Unfortunately, the powers of darkness have understood these principles far longer and far better than the Church. Therefore, satan has for a long time targeted key cities and has sought to control them so that from these key cities he can spiritually rule whole regions over which these cities have authority and influence.

Led by the Spirit of God, David did something in his day that was similar to what we have learned to do in India. He started with Jerusalem, the capital city. He took it completely and made it into an impregnable fortified city (see 2 Sam.

5:6-9). Then he went across the whole land of Israel and made every significant city into a fortified city. He put a garrison of his troops in each one that would secure the city and rule over the smaller communities and all the land on his behalf. (See 2 Sam. 5:6-9:13.)

Then he went into the land of the Philistines. He thoroughly defeated them in three very successful God-directed battles (see 2 Sam. 5:17-25). The Philistines then became subservient to him. He did not bother to occupy all their villages. He went straight to the major cities, took control of them, put a garrison there, and so exercised kingdom rule over the whole land. The villages had no power to resist him once he had control of the cities.

He then did the same thing with the Ammonites, the Moabites, the Edomites, the Amalekites, and all the other "ites" (see 2 Sam. 8:1-15). He took their cities, put garrisons in all the key cities, and so subdued the land. For the rest of his reign and well into the reign of Solomon, Israel never had any trouble from any of their enemies. They kept absolutely quiet for about 40 years. Throughout the kingdom, everybody enjoyed peace and prosperity.

In a similar way, if the Church is ever going to bring the Kingdom of God to a nation, it must first bring the Kingdom of God to the primary cities. If you are going to bring the government of God to a particular city, you must have a united, apostolically-led, warring church in that city.

In the natural, you cannot conquer a nation and overthrow a king by waging a guerilla war from a few of the villages. If there is a rebellion against the king in some of the villages, they may be able to harass the king somewhat and maybe even kill some of his soldiers. They can fight a guerilla war and have some limited, local success. But they cannot change the government without first taking charge of the major cities, especially the capital city.

I have watched the growth of the Charismatic movement over a number of decades. In 1925, there were about 7 million Spirit-filled believers worldwide, mainly in traditional Pentecostal churches. This growth sprang out of the revivals at the beginning of the 20th century.

Some amazing statistics are being published that should hearten everyone who is watching church growth. The World Christian Encyclopedia estimates the numbers of Pentecostal/Charismatic Christians in the world as follows:

- 1900 - 981,400

- 1970 - 72 million

- 1990 - 425 million

- 2000 - 524 million

- 2025 - 812 million

- 2050 - 1,066 million[4]

As I considered this vast increase of Spirit-filled believers worldwide, I had a problem because I didn't see our Western cities changing for the better spiritually. In fact, in Western countries, the cities particularly seemed to be getting much worse. Spiritually, they were much darker in spite of all these new believers supposedly anointed with power.

So I asked God, "Lord, what's the problem? Why haven't we impacted the cities, and why are we not changing our society? In fact everything seems to be getting worse."

The Lord said to me, "The reason is because you are building the wrong kind of churches. What you are doing spiritually is building little local, individual, autonomous 'village' churches, and they have no power to enter the heavens and change the environment over the cities, and therefore, they cannot rule the nation. You must concentrate, as David and the early Church did, on building city churches, which become strong regional and apostolic centers. Only this kind of church is capable of spiritually taking over the cities and impacting the region."

When Jesus sent out the group of 70 (some manuscripts say 72) He sent them *"into every city and place where He Himself was about to go"* (Luke 10:1). When

Paul went to break open a new region, he always went first to the major city of that region and then trained the new city church to reach the rest of the region themselves (see Acts 16-19).

In First Thessalonians 1:2-8 we see a great example of this. When Paul arrived in Thessalonica, he was only able to stay for three weeks before he was driven out of the city by an angry mob of hostile Jews (see Acts 17:1-10). But in that short time, he was able to preach to the idol-worshiping pagans of that city with such effect that they turned from their idols to serve the living God.

In the first two chapters of this wonderful letter of Paul, we learn that they received him for who he really was: a messenger (biblical text says an *angel* of God in Galatians 4:14). They received his word for what it really was, the Word of God. As a result, this Word was able to do its work in them because they believed. They became imitators of Paul and of the Lord (see 2 Thess. 2:14; note the Greek word *mimetes*[5]) and were soon shaking the whole region of Macedonia and Achaia with mighty miracles—so much so that Paul essentially declared, "From you the whole region is being reached, so we do not need to say anything" (see 1 Thess. 1:5-8).

A SPIRITUAL VILLAGE

What is a spiritual village? It is a typical local church working largely on its own. It may have 50-300 people meeting together in isolation with a senior pastor and some elders as their government. This pastor and his leaders spiritually represent a self-contained village. At best, all they can do is wage a guerilla war against the devil and his demons, but they cannot think of spiritually taking over society.

They may succeed in casting out a few demons, see a few people healed and get a few people saved, but they do not change the balance of power in the heavens. Nor can they change their city or see any kind of significant transformation.

Because of their independence, these thousands of new charismatic churches have been fighting a guerilla war and not a strategic war. We need to learn from Scripture and hear from the Holy Spirit about how to change this situation.

What God primarily trained the first apostles to do was to concentrate on certain strategic major cities in which they would plant churches and then build the growing number of congregations into a powerful regional center or city church.

Jerusalem was the first one. Antioch was the next. Thessalonica and Ephesus followed soon afterward. These all became powerful regional centers, and they were all characterized by a plurality of apostles, prophets, and other Ephesians 4:11 ministries in each place. Their governments did not consist of a local pastor with a group of elders around him, but a leading apostle who had other apostles, prophets, and Ephesians 4:11 ministries gathered around him. This one lead apostle had a humble servant heart, but exercised a clear headship role amongst them. The measure of their gift and faith was to build something much bigger and more powerful than a local church. They became regional centers and built one city church with many congregations.

If we hear God and let the Holy Spirit do what He wants in our cities, then all the qualities of David's government will be reproduced in them today. That means we would again reproduce what they had in the early Church and have the same city-transforming power and impact they had. Planting any number of little local "village" churches will have some effect, but we will never change society working that way.

If we will work together in the right way, we can build regional centers of incredible power that will be capable of transforming the cities and regions in which they are established *and* have spiritual authority. With such a strategy, we will begin to see the transformation of whole regions and even nations.

If we really want His Kingdom to come, we must stop playing our little village-church games. We must be prepared to learn new things from God. It is a great start to live in His presence and have wonderful times of intimacy with Him, but even that is not enough.

We must obey His Word, do His will, do His works, understand His ways, and be ready to fight His wars. God has great plans and strategies for the nations in which we live and to which He wants to send us.

CITY CHURCH / REGIONAL CENTER QUALITIES

A city church should be a proclamation and demonstration of the vision of the apostolic team that resides there. It needs to include:

1. *A group of apostolic men and women* with a recognized leader among them, so that they can truly become an apostolic center. The city church or regional center is a rich resource center with all the Ephesians 4:11 ministries functioning together.

2. *Prophetic men and women* who can prophesy God's vision and strategize with the apostles to determine the God-given practical steps to fulfill that vision.

3. *A gathering of the other Ephesians 4:11 ministries*, namely evangelists, pastors, and teachers who are under apostolic government and will work with the apostles and prophets to fulfill the vision. The fundamental life of the city church is fueled by prayer so that a *fully developed apostolic prayer center, functioning like David's tabernacle,* becomes a powerhouse that drives all ministry that goes out from the center. *Such a city church will have a group of satellite local churches* in the wider region that relate to it, but are not functionally part of it on a daily basis.

Although the satellite churches would be too far away to be functionally part of the city church, they would remain in good relationship to the apostolic ministries in the city church and would receive regular visits from the apostolic team and their delegates. They would endeavor to come and participate in the special events of the city church. These local churches would grow in numbers and maturity from the input they regularly receive from the apostles and prophets and other Ephesians 4:11 ministries (and their delegates) of the city church.

In Appendix A, I have included many details that I believe should be developed to produce an effective city church.

GOVERNMENT IN THE CITY CHURCH

The government of the city church is under the leadership of an apostle with a group of other apostles working together with prophets, the other Ephesians 4:11 ministries, and the elders.

In matters relating to strategy, foundation-laying, or planting and building churches, the apostles work with the prophets (see Eph. 2:20-3:5). In major decisions affecting the lives of the people, they would consult with the elders of the city church as well as the apostles (see Acts 15:4-6).

A fully-formed city church would have a plurality of apostles just as a local church has a plurality of elders. In Jerusalem there were initially 12 apostles, but that number increased when James, the brother of Jesus, plus some others were also recognized as apostles. Whenever apostles are mentioned functionally in the New Testament, they are always in the plural (see Acts 4:33, 37, 5:12, 6:6, 8:14, 9:27, 16:4; Eph. 3:5; 2 Pet. 3:2; etc.). Although there was a plurality of apostles in Jerusalem, James was recognized as having the final authority among them. He was very humble and consulted everybody over the decision made by the first council in Jerusalem as to whether the new Gentile believers should be circumcised and keep the Jewish Law. This is recorded in Acts chapter 15:1-29.

To form a present-day city church or regional center, the local churches in one city or region need to come into closer relationship with one another. They must then recognize and come under one overall apostolic government so there will be no dividing walls between them. This builds one mighty, impregnable, spiritual wall of fire around the outside of the whole city that completely protects them all from any external demonic attack (see Zech. 2:4-5).

Each church member should have a loyal commitment to his own local church. However, there should also be a clear sense of identity with the whole city and a definite commitment to be actively involved in citywide events. Physically, from time to time, the whole city church should meet together so that the leaders and the people have unity of purpose. It is necessary to actually see the entirety of the whole as more important than anyone's own individual part of it.

City churches have the power to impact the whole of society and bring about a fulfillment of Psalms 2 as we saw in Acts 4:24-35. These New Testament city churches threatened the existing demonic rulers over the city and had the authority and power to overcome them and cast them down.

UNIQUE IMPACT OF CITY CHURCH LIFE

When the Church in Jerusalem was born on the Day of Pentecost, it rapidly became a great spiritual group comprised of many thousands and possessed all the qualities of city church life as described above and in Appendix A.

Its unique impact can be summarized as follows:

- It was visible and could not be hidden (see Matt. 5:14-16).

- It was powerful, with many signs and wonders taking place (see Matt. 4:23-25).

- It had much larger resources than a local church for prayer, evangelism, operational gifts and ministries, and finances.

- It provided a more suitable home base for apostles, prophets, teachers, pastors, and evangelists, one from which they went out to serve the churches in the region and beyond.

- It also provided a suitable platform for visiting Ephesians 4:11 ministries to touch the whole city effectively, in one visit.

- It had the power to influence and exercise authority in secular society.

- It could realistically strategize to evangelize the region, the nation, and other nations of the world.

- It could exercise spiritual rule over the region and clear the heavens of the demonic powers in the heavenly realm.

BOUNDARIES OF SPIRITUAL AND NATURAL CITIES

Spiritual and natural city boundaries differ. While a significant population is necessary to provide the numbers for a city church, the physical limits of a spiritual city do not necessarily coincide with the boundaries of an actual physical one. In some of the gigantic modern cities we have today, it may work a lot better, in terms of having real relationships, to form several spiritual cities within one physical city. The practical limits of a spiritual city are flexible and depend upon the heart, mindset, and possibly the culture and ethnicity of the people. It would depend on their ability and willingness to maintain real, living relationships and their willingness to travel in order to meet regularly.

Today, in regions where there are no nearby sizable cities, a number of smaller towns and communities have successfully banded together over an area of 10 to 20 miles to form an effective, functionally successful regional church. This is well established in what happened in Andhra Pradesh, India, as further described in this book. There is no set formula for how large or small boundaries should be for a city or regional church to cover. It is dependent on the willingness of the apostolic leaders and churches to come into one heart and mind in order to work together for the Kingdom.

ENDNOTES

1. *Biblesoft's New Exhaustive Strong's Numbers and Concordance with Expanded Greek-Hebrew Dictionary*. CD-ROM. Biblesoft, Inc. and International Bible Translators, Inc. (© 1994, 2003, 2006), s.v. "Apostello," (NT 649).

2. *Blue Letter Bible,* "Dictionary and Word Search for *apostolos* (Strong's 652)," 1996-2011, < http://www.blueletterbible.org/lang/lexicon/lexicon.cfm?strongs=G652> (accessed June 8, 2011).

3. *Biblesoft's New Exhaustive Strong's Numbers and Concordance*, s.v. "Basileia," (NT 932).

4. David B. Barrett, George T. Kurian, and Todd M. Johnson, eds., *World Christian Encyclopedia: A Comparative Survey of Churches and Religions in The Modern World, 2nd ed.,* (Oxford University Press, USA, 2001), 4.

5. *Biblesoft's New Exhaustive Strong's Numbers and Concordance*, s.v. "Mimetes," (NT 3402).

CHAPTER 6

A WORKING CITY CHURCH

JUST as we have explored the dynamics of the larger city or regional church, it is equally important to provide insight into how smaller local churches make up the whole of the larger church. The individual local churches or "villages" of the city church consist of congregations or communities comprising about 100 to 400 people in each. All of these are within one city church. Each congregation is made up of a number of home groups.

The church in the city meets regularly in three different ways. This gives all the people the opportunity to function in ministry and be enriched in their lives as they meet in each of these different formats. Let us now look at each of them in more detail.

FIRST: HOME GROUPS

Home groups meet regularly, usually on a weekly basis. Visitors and friends should always be welcome. These home groups concentrate on making new contacts in their immediate neighborhood and, as a first priority, bringing new contacts to a saving knowledge of Jesus as Lord. These meetings also provide an opportunity to meet personal needs, heal the sick, and pray for one another as well as take up wider issues in prayer. This leads to deepening personal relationships and enables all individuals to be properly pastored so as to bring them to maturity. It is also a place for individuals to learn how to move in all the gifts of the Spirit and for God to come and move uniquely in any way He desires.

Presenting a message or having a set teaching time could occur, if judged profitable by the leader. The home group provides a forum to study a teaching or a particular topic that the senior pastor might be emphasizing for the whole church. For these reasons it should have order and leadership. There should be freedom for the Holy Spirit to move as He chooses and for everybody to have the liberty to participate as the Spirit of God indicates.

It is clear from the first two chapters of the Book of Acts that the early Church in Jerusalem had all these different forms of meeting together. Acts 2:41-47 explains:

> *Then those who gladly received his word were baptized; and that day about three thousand souls were added to them. And they continued steadfastly in the apostles' doctrine and fellowship, in the breaking of bread, and in prayers. Then fear came upon every soul, and many wonders and signs were done through the apostles. Now all who believed were together, and had all things in common, and sold their possessions and goods, and divided them among all, as anyone had need. So continuing daily with one accord in the temple, and breaking bread from house to house, they ate their food with gladness and simplicity of heart, praising God and having favor with all the people. And the Lord added to the church daily those who were being saved.*

SECOND: LOCAL CHURCH CONGREGATIONAL MEETINGS

Weekly congregational meetings in the immediate locality should be held (usually on Sunday mornings) in a suitable building ideally capable of holding about twice the number of the committed membership of that congregation.

The meeting should begin with a great time of extravagant worship, prayer, and moving in the gifts of the Spirit. Unless God leads otherwise, there should normally be a definite time of teaching from the Word of God. The members should also have an opportunity to bring their tithes and offerings to the Lord as part of their extravagant worship. This kind of meeting, as well as being the main means to edify the whole body, also provides an opportunity to develop the gifts within the body—in worship leaders, prayer leaders, prophets, pastors, evangelists, and teachers, as well as in musicians, healing gifts and miracle-workers, children and youth workers, and so forth. Apart from the teaching time, the children and young people should be fully involved and freely participate in the main meeting as the Spirit of God leads them.

A person with final leadership authority over the meeting should be open and sensitive to whatever the Holy Spirit is saying and be willing to let God move in any way He chooses. For that reason, meetings should not be too structured or overly organized. At the same time, everything should be done with a sense of Kingdom excellence and proper order. The leader should aim to complete the meeting punctually, within a reasonable time frame, without quenching the Holy Spirit. The proper leading of such a meeting requires great sensitivity and skill. As part of the life of the church, regular training to develop such leaders should be ongoing.

THIRD: CELEBRATION MEETINGS

Every few months, the whole city church should come together in a large public auditorium. Such gatherings present an opportunity for times of extravagant worship where the best of the worship leaders, musicians, and singers from all the local churches could be utilized to form a special band to lead these meetings. Also, such a meeting provides a chance to hear the city church's apostolic leader or a visiting speaker. Visitors should be publicly invited to commit their lives to Christ. A capable group of ministries should be at hand, ready to minister to all who come forward at the close of the meeting for salvation, healing, and other needs. In addition, two major citywide conferences should be planned each year to encourage and "re-envision" the church.

Various specialty training and teaching programs should be in place. These should be available for everybody in the whole city church and aimed at developing all the gift potential across the entire body. Every local church should commit itself as a whole congregation to be part of these city events and recognize that these events would always have the priority over their local programs.

The qualities and functions for a local church within the city church are listed in Appendix B.

THE CITY CHURCH FULFILLS ACTS 1:8

When Jesus rose from the dead, He sent out His apostles to be witnesses—first, in their own hometown; second, to their own nation; then to the adjacent nations; and finally, to the uttermost parts of the earth (see Acts 1:8).

This commission was given primarily to the apostles when they were alone with Jesus, but it had to involve the whole Body of Christ in its outworking. It was the particular responsibility of these apostles to see that this commandment was fulfilled. Local elders and local churches, once they are "envisioned," can pool their resources to fulfill that commission. Therefore, a city church with a plurality of apostolic ministries and many local churches together can more realistically respond to the call.

Now let us examine the Acts 1:8 call more closely.

1) "Jerusalem"—Picture of the Home City

To reach "our Jerusalem" would mean planting new local churches in new communities within the geographical boundaries of the present city church. These new local churches would then become part of the one city church. From the beginning, they would receive full support from all the resources of the city church and would grow without any sense of isolation.

TWO WAYS TO PLANT NEW LOCAL CHURCHES:

a) From an existing local church. After a local church has been established for some time, we often find a group of believers may begin to attend that church from an adjacent area which is some distance away. They are drawn by the life and fellowship this local church provides. However, it may become hard for them to be fully involved because of the distance and travel time. It is also difficult to persuade their friends, relatives, and contacts in their own area to make the journey to the distant church and even harder to have any significant impact upon their own community.

To solve these issues, a new local church can be planted using this existing company of believers as the foundational core group of the new work in their immediate geographical area. This is what I have come to call the "strawberry plant" principle. The elders of the existing local church must agree to maintain oversight over the newly planted church during its early days. They must also supply whatever gifted ministries are necessary until the planted church has reached maturity and has all these ministries available from within itself.

Then local elders should be appointed in the planted church and the governmental ties of the "mother church" severed, leaving strong relational ties in place. The new church would at all times firmly remain part of the city church and continue under the overall apostolic government of that city.

b) By direct planting out into a new, unreached area. In this case the apostles, prophets, and evangelists from the city church would receive direct revelation from God concerning an area in which there is no existing community of believers. They would then direct an evangelistic thrust into the target area to produce a group of new converts from which the new church would grow. During the growth period, eldership oversight would be provided from a nearby local church. Once the new church was established and had developed mature elders of its own, the governmental ties would be cut and only the relational ties would remain. The newly planted church would remain firmly planted as a part of the city church and would continue under its apostolic government.

The goal of a city church should be to have at least one functioning local church in every significant community over the entire geographical region for which it has responsibility.

2) "Judea"—Picture of the Home Nation

Going to Judea, the home nation, would mean planting churches beyond the region where the city church is situated, but within its own national frontiers. The aim would be to eventually raise up new city churches and provide new bases for apostles and Ephesians 4:11 ministries across the nation. In this way, a network of strong city churches would be established gradually, to provide covering and exercise spiritual government to a broader national base.

Apostolic ministries from existing city churches would exercise fatherly governmental authority over these embryonic city churches during their formative years. But when they reach maturity, the governmental ties would again be cut to leave only relational ties. While these different apostolic centers would have strong relationships among them and work together in partnership, particularly over state and national issues, no one center would permanently exercise any governmental control over any other.

It would also be necessary to plant many new local churches in the surrounding smaller communities. Not all local churches are destined to become city churches. It is unrealistic to have or imply that expectation. When new churches seem destined to remain as solid local churches, then they need to be plugged into the nearest city church and draw the benefits of city life from that source to avoid becoming too local and parochial in their outlook.

Established city churches need to be prepared to serve the local churches of the region and beyond, including those that are not integrally part of them. In this way, the big city churches can give the surrounding local churches the blessing and encouragement of their strong city life. It must be done in a spirit of genuine servanthood, seeking only to serve and not to annex or take ownership. In this way, the city churches can run Bible weeks, conventions, Bible schools, internships, training programs, and so forth for the whole region and beyond, thereby greatly enriching the entire body in that region.

3) "Samaria"—Picture of Surrounding Nations

Like the early Church, our goal in preaching the Kingdom to every nation must be to evangelize these nations and to establish effective indigenous city churches within them. These would provide a suitable base for emerging apostolic teams and would develop autonomous apostolic and prophetic ministry.

When we go to surrounding nations, we should be looking for key people with apostolic and prophetic potential within those nations, as well as evangelizing the people at large. Once again, these developing apostolic ministries and the embryonic city churches would remain under the oversight of mature apostles and developed city churches until they come to maturity. Then the governmental ties would be cut, but the loving relational ties and servant attitudes would always remain.

4) "The Uttermost Parts of the Earth"

The strategy for this part of the commission is exactly the same as for the surrounding nations, except that these apostles and their teams may travel to any part of the world as God directs them. Some city churches or regional centers have a call from God to serve many different nations in this way. The goal is always to identify local indigenous apostles, prophets, and other Ephesians 4:11 ministries and teach and train them until indigenous apostolic teams and full-grown city churches are established in that nation.

DIFFERENT APOSTLES HAVE DIFFERENT SPHERES

As we have seen in Acts 1:8, Jesus gave this fourfold commission to the first group of apostles who were sent to go and preach the Kingdom to every creature on the face of the earth. But there was specialization even within this first team. Not everyone was to go everywhere; they were only to go where they were sent. Remember the word *apostle* simply means "a sent one." Even among the first 12, they were given different spheres.

1) The Jerusalem Apostle—James the Example

Some apostles have a call to stay home, build, and then oversee the regional city church as James did in Jerusalem. There is no record of him traveling widely as Peter and Paul did. Today there are "Jerusalem" apostles just like James, who stay home and concentrate on building apostolic regional centers. Such apostles are not called primarily to be pastors, but to draw all the Ephesians 4:11 ministries together and get them working as a powerful team.

2) The Judean Apostle—Peter the Example

Other apostles are called to the nation of their birth and to the people of their own language and ethnicity; they do not usually travel much beyond their own national boundaries to people of other cultures. Peter, who was called to his own people, the Jews, is a great biblical example of this kind of apostle.

3) The Samaritan Apostle—Philip the Example

Others are called only to the surrounding adjacent nations. This is true of Philip, a Jew, who went to Samaria. It would be similar to an American going to Canada or Mexico; or to those from England going to France, Italy, or Germany. They often speak a common language and have a similar common culture to the nations to which they are called.

4) The Whole-Earth Apostle—Paul the Example

For the apostles who are called to many nations, the whole world becomes their parish. They travel internationally and are rarely at home. The city church or apostolic regional center can provide a base for all these differing apostolic ministries and often, a home church family for traveling apostles and their natural families to belong to. From this base, they go out and return, like Paul and

Barnabas did to Antioch. This regional center is also often the place that regularly prays for and supports their ministries.

In the city churches or regional centers, there will be a plurality of apostles and other Ephesians 4:11 ministries. In the company of other apostolic and prophetic peers, all four kinds of apostles find encouragement, "envisioning," mutual strengthening, and accountability. They are secure among those who can understand and monitor their ministries. It is not good or biblically correct for any minister to walk alone, even if he is an apostle.

APOSTLES: KNOW YOUR MINISTRY, SPHERE, AND MEASURE

Many times in the Gospels, Jesus rebuked those first apostles for arguing, discussing, or disputing among themselves about which of them was going to be the greatest in the Kingdom. Several times He set a little child in their midst and commanded them all to become like that little child. If they wanted to be great in the Kingdom, they were to become like little children and be the servants of all (see Matt. 18:1-4; Luke 22:24-27).

In Second Corinthians 10:12-18, Paul, first of all, strongly condemned those who sought to make a name for themselves and who kept comparing themselves with one another to see who was the greatest. He made it very clear that we should know the sphere that God has appointed us to and not seek to go beyond it. If we do, we will be in disobedience and may interfere with and hinder what God is already doing through another apostolic ministry.

Second, we should only seek to function at our true measure and not try to be, or make ourselves out to be, bigger in God than we are really are.

Third, we should know what God has called us to be and to do in our particular ministry. We should have a very clear job description. Paul said of himself that he was called to be an apostle, preacher, and teacher to the Gentiles (see 1 Tim. 2:7; 2 Tim. 1:11) and to make known to them *the unsearchable riches of Christ*"(Eph. 3:8).

Paul was equally emphatic that even though he was a Jew and had a great burden for the Jews, they were no longer part of his sphere. He recognized that Peter and James were now specifically called to be apostles to the Jews (see Rom. 9:1-5, 11:26; Gal. 2:7-9).

THE KINGDOM AND MISSIONS BEGAN WITH JERUSALEM

The resurrection commandment Jesus gave to His disciples to go into all the world, preach the Gospel to every creature, and make disciples of all nations (see Mark 16:15; Matt. 28:18-20) was not immediately obeyed.

It took persecution following the martyrdom of Stephen for the church in Jerusalem to begin to fulfill this command. It began with Jerusalem, the first and only city church at that time. From there it went to Samaria, then to the Gentile household of Cornelius, and on to Antioch, which became the first Gentile city to be really touched.

When the report came back to Jerusalem that the Spirit had fallen on Gentiles just as He had on Jews in the upper room on the Day of Pentecost, they began to obey Jesus' commandment more earnestly. They then sent out apostolic teams to plant new churches and form new apostolic centers, or city churches.

ANTIOCH: THE NEXT APOSTOLIC CENTER

Soon, Antioch became an apostolic center in its own right and a gathering place for several apostles and prophets and all other Ephesians 4:11 ministries. Antioch then began to send out its own apostolic teams to evangelize and plant churches in totally new areas. These apostolic teams reported back to Antioch and not to Jerusalem (see Acts 14:26-28).

JERUSALEM AND ANTIOCH:
A NON-CONTROLLING PARTNERSHIP

The apostles in Jerusalem were in relationship with those in Antioch. They consulted each other, but never directed or controlled what the other was doing. Antioch concentrated on the Gentile world while Jerusalem sent apostles to the many Jewish communities scattered all over the Roman Empire and beyond.

First Thessalonica, and then Ephesus, became city churches. Antioch gave birth to Thessalonica; later a powerful center was established in Ephesus. These rapidly became city churches and apostolic regional centers in their own right with many churches that they themselves had planted. The new churches were under the direct apostolic care of the apostles who planted them and of the apostolic centers that originally sent apostolic teams out.

The original apostolic centers were soon actively giving birth to other new apostolic centers. The clear strategy was to evangelize and then identify and develop the indigenous apostles, prophets, and other Ephesians 4:11 ministries in the new region. The founding apostle with his team of other ministries would then father these embryonic apostles and other ministries to maturity. They were then released to build their own strongly related, but not externally controlled, apostolic centers and city churches in their own cities and nations.

All mission activity was apostolically envisioned and directed.

In the early Church, all missionaries went out in apostolic teams led or directed by apostles. These missionaries were either apostles themselves or were sent as apostolic delegations to serve a particular apostle. The apostolic delegations were sent either from the home base of the apostle whom they went to serve or to an apostle who, though from a different home base, was already established in the region to which the delegation was going. Individual missionaries doing their own independent thing were unknown in those days.

Whatever was established was put into local hands as soon as indigenous apostles had emerged and these new regional apostolic centers had become mature enough to handle their own affairs. They were not controlled from some international headquarters, and they did not carry some worldwide international or denominational label such as "The Jerusalem World Outreach Church in Antioch."

Financial and other practical support continued to flow from one region to another so that one region's wealth could minister to another region's lack. But it was placed at the local apostles' feet, and these apostles were then responsible for handling these resources with wisdom, humility, and complete financial integrity.

"PARA-CHURCH" MINISTRIES: VALIDITY AND ROLES

We need to see that God's plan and desire is to have one Church, one Body, one family, in each city working and serving together as members one of another. Even though we might meet in separate communities for our regular Sunday meetings, we are still part of one another.

Once we see this, we understand that no legitimate ministry raised up by God can truly be called a para-church ministry. *Para-church* literally means working outside or alongside the Church, which was never God's plan. Every ministry must see itself and be recognized as being within the one Body of Christ and part of the one Church. Each ministry should support, recognize, and have relationships with and accountability to the God-appointed leadership and apostolic authorities in the city. Such ministries are raised up by God to fulfill a specific function of the one Body of Christ. There is only one *ecclesia* or community of believers in any city.

If our perspective is totally centered on our own local church and if we are totally focused on only doing our own local thing, then we may wrongly see some of these ministries as being outside of us or at best alongside us. But they should always be seen as part of us.

Some are called to "the Church" and some are called to "the work." This distinction between "the Church" and "the work" was a favorite expression of

Watchman Nee as he tried to make this difference clear. He carefully distinguished between serving God directly in the life of a local church and serving God in the wider apostolic work of establishing and extending the Kingdom of God, whether in the city or in other regions and nations.

In this sense, many apostles and other Ephesians 4:11 ministries are called to the work of the Kingdom and to the wider Church Body and cannot at the same time be too deeply involved in the daily life of any single local community of believers or local church.

When a local church can joyfully see this, then they can be a non-demanding family base for the people who are called to "the work." Those called to "the work" and their families can be prayed for, supported, and refreshed within the local community without that community putting unreasonable demands on their time, gifts, or finances.

In doing this, the community actively sows into the wider work of the Kingdom and, as Jesus promised, will receive their reward from the Lord.

Let's cry out:

> *Lord, You have plans that are exactly right for our political, social, and economic situations in this nation; and they are exactly right for our spiritual condition. Lord, we want to be as wise as David. We want to be united with the other leaders whom You have raised up. We want to seek Your face together with Your apostles, prophets, and other Ephesians 4:11 ministries. Together, we want to all hear from God. We want them to know that it is of You. We want them to know that it is good.*

> *We ask that all of Your people receive a vision that is good for the whole of the Body of Christ. Then we will abandon the futile and useless ways learned from our fathers or invented ourselves; we will start to do Your will with Your power so that the Kingdom You have promised will come in its fullness, and all our enemies will be defeated. We will reap a mighty harvest, the glory of Your Church will increase, the power of Your government will increase, and all society will be impacted and changed. We*

believe that You are sufficient to do this. We are willing. We are available to do Your will. Lord, let Your Kingdom come. Let Your will truly be done on Earth, just as it is in Heaven, in Jesus' mighty name. Amen!

CHAPTER 7

ESTABLISHING JERUSALEM—
THE HEAVENLY CITY

ABRAHAM received a commandment to leave his hometown of Ur of the Chaldeans and go on a long journey. As it says in Hebrews 11:8, he obeyed by faith, not knowing where he was going.

In the Book of Genesis, chapters 12 to 22, we read of another great journey that Abraham and Sarah accomplished at the same time. This was an amazing spiritual journey of faith that was destined to change their names prophetically. It also completely changed Abraham's life and made him a different person; he became the father of all those who believe, Jew and Gentile alike.

This journey is briefly summarized in Romans 4:17-21. Verse 20 literally says that Abraham was "empowered"[1] with faith to believe that Sarah would have a child by him who would be the beginning of the multitudes. Hebrews 11:11 says that Sarah was empowered with faith in order to conceive that child. The Greek word used in each case is *dunamis*[2] or one of its derivatives. These words are the basis of our English words *power, dynamic,* and *dynamite*. The remarkable faith Abraham and Sarah exercised didn't come from within them at all, but was imparted into their awakened human spirits as a gift straight from the very Spirit of God.

The highlights of this journey of faith are also recorded for us in Hebrews 11:17-19. There we read that Abraham believed that even if he had killed Isaac and offered him as a sacrifice in obedience to God's command, he would nevertheless receive him back from the dead so as to fulfill God's promise that through Isaac a multitude of descendants as numerous as the stars would come from his loins. As this promise could not fail, both Abraham and Isaac were already in faith to believe for Isaac's resurrection before Abraham moved to plunge the knife into him. This act of faith sealed the fullness of Abraham's inheritance.

As God walked with Abraham on that long journey from Ur of the Chaldeans to the Promised Land, He showed him many things and enabled him to begin to see the magnitude of His great Kingdom purposes. We cannot go into all the detail this deserves, but we must, at least, look at the highlights.

THE CITY

As I stated in the Introduction, some of us were robbed for years by the theology we were taught. Our expectation for the present was taken away from us completely by wrongly relegating the fulfillment of many great prophetic events until after the return of Christ. Now we are seeing that there can be at least a partial, present fulfillment of many of these things, although the full final glory may have to wait until Jesus' return when the new Heaven and the new earth are established.

Until recently, most of the Church believed that the manifestation of the heavenly city of Jerusalem was a future event. This city would suddenly appear out of Heaven as a bride adorned for her husband as part of the Second Coming of Jesus, having had no previous existence or relevance.

As I discuss in the following paragraphs, God is now revealing that the heavenly city of Jerusalem came into existence on the Day of Pentecost. It was first established in the spirit realm over the earthly city of Jerusalem at the same time that the Church was born and began to pray in that upper room.

This heavenly city became effective as a powerful heavenly influence from those first days of the Church. It was the power of that spiritual city that shook the principalities and powers of darkness over Jerusalem and cast them down. Those demonic spirits had long ago formed a spiritual canopy over the physical city of Jerusalem on earth. From that polluted heavenly realm, they were able to rule over the religious system and so control the minds of most of the people who lived in Jerusalem. These demonic powers had strongly opposed the ministry of Jesus on earth and had been able to restrict much of the manifestation of the Kingdom while He was on earth throughout His ministry. This continued until He broke the power of these spirits at the cross and was raised up in triumph by the glory of the Father to rule over them all.

Once the Church was born and heavenly Jerusalem was established, the saints in Jerusalem were able to wrest from these demonic powers the spiritual government in the heavenly realm over the physical city of Jerusalem. The result was that this demonic canopy of darkness over Jerusalem was removed, and the whole spiritual climate changed on Earth. As a direct result, many spiritually-blind and demonically-hardened people in that city came under deep conviction and repented of their terrible sin. They had refused Jesus as their King and crucified Him instead. Gratefully receiving His forgiveness, they put their trust in Him as their King and Savior and were baptized. This became a massive ingathering of souls into the Kingdom of God, with multitudes being added to the Church every day. The church in Jerusalem rapidly grew to about 20,000 members within two years.

ABRAHAM SAW A CITY

We are told in Scripture that Abraham and others spiritually saw a city which had foundations whose builder and maker was God (see Heb. 11:8-10, 13-16). He saw this city afar off and embraced it although he never saw its actual manifestation during his lifetime on earth.

Somehow God showed Abraham that this city was vital to the fulfilling of His promise to him that he and his descendants would inherit and rule with Jesus over the whole earth and not just the Holy Land (see Rom. 4:13).

Abraham was promised the power to become a great nation as numerous as the stars in heaven. He also believed he would be the father of many nations and be able to bless all the families of the earth (see Gen. 12:1-3). He lived in Canaan, the land of promise, as an alien or sojourner (see Heb. 11:9). He had no desire to return to Ur of the Chaldeans, nor did he have any intention of settling permanently in Canaan, for he had seen another "country"—that is, a heavenly one.

Somehow God showed him that the only way to take over the world was for his descendants to first spiritually occupy and then exercise rule from that heavenly realm over the earth. To do this, spiritual cities were necessary. These cities alone have the strength and firepower to overcome and cast out the demonic princes, which in most cases are the well-established present rulers, or powers of the air, presiding over most cities in the world. These demonic princes long ago had spread their influence upon the earth and now ruled the present darkness from their well-established heavenly vantage points.

Another thing Abraham saw was that the multitude of descendants God had promised him, as numerous as the stars in the heavens, would be gathered in once this rule of darkness was smashed and replaced by the rule of the Kingdom of God. That does not mean that everybody would automatically be saved or that the demonic powers would altogether cease their activities, but many more people would be freed to turn from darkness to light once the canopy of darkness over our cities was lifted.

Again, I believe that Abraham saw that the heavenly city was crucial to the change of rule and that it would cause men and women to be saved in unprecedented numbers. So Abraham saw: a *land*, a *multitude*, and a *city*. But it was the city that would be the means to possess the land and reap the multitude.

JERUSALEM WAS THAT CITY

The language of some of our church theology and hymnology is still looking forward to the day when a "new" Jerusalem will appear, after Christ's return. This is still the theology of many Christians. But, as stated above, the new heavenly Jerusalem already existed while the New Testament was being written and actually came into existence the moment the Church was born on the Day of Pentecost.

However, some great hymns and patriotic songs were written during past revivals in the time of these great evangelists, John and Charles Wesley, in which these truths were seen, taught, written, and sung. One such example is the poem entitled "Jerusalem" by William Blake and set to music by Charles Parry in the late 19th Century. The writer is longing for heavenly Jerusalem to be built "in England's green and pleasant land"[3] through effective spiritual warfare.

The final glory of that city will only be seen when she finally comes down out of Heaven in all her glory adorned as a bride for her husband at the end of the age (see Rev. 21:1-2, 9-27). But that does not mean that she does not already exist in the heavenly realm and is not already able to function powerfully when we have the faith and vision to work with God and His angels to make it happen. May we sing that same song that William Blake wrote and pray that same prayer for the cities anywhere in the world where we are geographically located.

WILL IT EVER HAPPEN?

I began to see these truths a long time ago. As the years have gone by, they have come to greater clarity. It was during a long fast that I first began to see that building the heavenly city of Jerusalem spiritually over a region or a particular physical city on Earth was the means that God had given for powerfully advancing the Kingdom of God.

Shortly afterward, I was privileged to speak on what God had shown me concerning heavenly Jerusalem at a major leaders' conference in England. There was a warm, excited response to the vision, and many were amazed at how much there was in Scripture about this heavenly city and the possibility of its present manifestation in some measure over our cities here on earth long before Jesus returns at the end of the age.

But when it was all over and people began to think through all the practicalities of actually making this happen, it seemed that the obstacles were insurmountable. The general response was that it was a very interesting concept, but not very practical. Most leaders felt that it was impossible for them to make the necessary change to produce a functioning regional or city church as described. They believed they were too far down the road in the wrong direction because of their existing church structure. No one was willing to make such a radical turnaround.

I remember walking away from that conference feeling very disappointed and saying to God, "I didn't dream this up myself. I know You put this into my heart, and I am prepared to go anywhere in the world to work with a group of leaders who seriously want to build this heavenly City of Jerusalem with its powerful ability to manifest a true city church on earth, just the way You have described it through the prophets in the Old and New Testament and have now shown it to me."

Some recent initiatives in different parts of the world have produced a portion of these qualities and to some extent are beginning to resemble what I saw. But I have not yet seen the whole thing brought together and fully functioning in the way God described it in all the various Scriptures He showed me. Nevertheless, I believe it must happen before Jesus returns. I am very encouraged by what I have seen beginning to happen in a few places in the world in the past decade.

I believe one day I will see it all, either while I am here on Earth or from Heaven after I have gone to glory. Either way, my heart cry is, "Come, Lord Jesus! Let Your Kingdom really come and invade this world with a glorious manifestation of Your Heaven on Earth!"

In these final days before Jesus comes again with His angels in all His glory, may we find a growing number of people full of faith, totally yielded to His

Spirit, actively cooperating with Him to establish the majesty of His glorious Kingdom.

May the local and international Church increasingly function like the Body of Christ. May this Church go to war like a mighty warrior as well as look more and more like His glorious Bride.

In all the nations of the earth, may we find God-centered, God-ordered, and God-directed battalions of the army of God effectively at war in the heavenly realm against the powers of darkness and at work on Earth preparing the way of the Lord.

A TALE OF TWO CITIES

In Paul's letter to the churches of Galatia, he speaks of the two cities of Jerusalem as being allegorically represented by the two children that Abraham had. His first child was through Hagar, Sarah's maid; the second was the miraculous child of promise, Isaac, whom Sarah finally bore by faith through Abraham when she was long past the age of natural childbearing.

Paul spoke of the present earthly city of Jerusalem of his day as being in the bondage of law with all her children (see Gal. 4:25). He clearly meant the existing physical city of Jerusalem on earth, which was characterized by the legalism and bondage of the religious Jewish leaders and their hatred of the name of Jesus and everything Christian. Even now, the present-day, physical Jerusalem continues to be the center of the legalism and deadness of three major world religions.

However, Paul also spoke of another Jerusalem that was heavenly. It was from above and, like Isaac, the child of promise, it came into existence through faith. He declared that she already existed in his day, was already free, and already was the mother of us all (see Gal. 4:26-28).

David declared in Psalm 87:5-6 that all real believers were born in this spiritual city of Jerusalem. For all the true children of promise, this city is in existence. It is where we were born, and it is where we are already living.

The writer of the great Book of Hebrews also speaks of this city. In Hebrews 12:18-24 the writer, inspired by the Holy Spirit, compares the two mountains with the two cities. One is Mount Sinai, with its fear, darkness, and bondage of religion. The other is Mount Zion, with its joy, light, liberty, and a multitude of dancing angels. As we are told in Hebrews 12:22-23: *"You have come to Mount Zion and to the city of the living God, the heavenly Jerusalem, to an innumerable company of angels, to the general assembly and church of the firstborn...."*

So where does the Church of born-again believers truly meet? The answer is in heavenly Jerusalem, which already is. This was the city that Abraham saw in his spirit, and he embraced it from afar although he never actually entered it during his lifetime on earth.

Abraham saw this city whose architect and builder was God. As born-again believers, we have the means of appropriating the power that rules in Heaven along with an innumerable company of angels to establish the Kingdom of God on earth. We can then go on to possess the whole world for King Jesus and reap a vast multitude of new believers.

JESUS SPEAKS OF *THE* CITY

In Matthew 5:13-15, Jesus said three things concerning the Church. He said it was to be salt, light, and a city that could not be hidden. Let us examine these three important components.

Salt—In the days when the Bible was written, salt was the main means of flavoring food and of preserving it, thereby stopping decay and corruption. In spiritual terms, Jesus was saying that the salt of the Kingdom was to permeate all of society with its flavor. In practice, individual Christians full of the power of the Kingdom would infiltrate every stratum of secular society, flavoring it with the joy, light, and righteousness of the Kingdom, thereby holding back the sin of darkness and the corruption that would otherwise completely swamp secular society.

Light—The light represents the life of the Kingdom shining with all its purity in an individual Christian, a Christian family, a truly Christian business, a Christian school, a Christian medical practice, or any "secular" institution in such a way that the true light of the Kingdom can shine forth without adulteration. As a result, it stands out as light against the darkness, in total contrast to the darkness, which is always present in similar institutions of this world. It gives a clear manifestation of the Kingdom for all to see.

City—This represents the powerful city churches from which the government of the Kingdom is to be established over the whole land. They cannot be hidden, but are known and can be seen for miles around by everybody.

BIG TREES AND SMALL BUSHES

Years ago God gave a vivid illustration to Eileen and me of the kind of regional city church He intended to build, especially in the last days. He used an illustration with which we were very familiar—a typical Indian tea garden, such as the ones found all over the Nilgiri Hills in Southern India and in Assam in Northern India. Tea grows on a bush that reaches a height of four feet. The bud and the first two small leaves on each twig are picked to make the best tea leaves. Although a hot climate is needed to grow tea, it grows best in the shade, and the bush struggles to survive if it is constantly exposed to the burning power of direct sunlight. For this reason, tall, shady trees are planted between the tea bushes to provide shade for them. As these trees grow in a mature tea garden, their branches spread out and touch each other to provide continuous shade to the tea bushes underneath. Under their protective shade, all the tea bushes are able to flourish.

God said He wanted city churches or regional centers like we saw in the early Church to arise again like the big trees in the tea gardens. These city churches would serve all of their aligned local churches and give them shade and protection from demonic attacks so that they could all flourish and grow just like the tea bushes in the tea garden under the shade of the big trees.

In Matthew 13:31-32, Jesus taught that the Kingdom of God is like a mustard seed that, contrary to nature, grows into a great tree. As it rises into the heavens and spreads out its branches, it gives shade and protection to the whole region. God showed me that this "mustard tree" was an allegorical picture of these great city churches, which would spiritually function like the protective trees in the tea garden, giving protection to all the local churches and causing them to flourish. The birds that nest in the branches were symbolic of angels being much more actively involved in the life of the churches because these city churches facilitate their involvement.

Among the many new churches that are springing up all over the place, certain of them are destined to grow into powerful spiritual city churches. These churches will have the ability and authority to penetrate the heavens and then exercise regional rule in the heavenly realm over the powers of darkness—for the benefit of all the churches in that region.

When these spiritual "mustard trees" have grown up all around the nation, their branches will spread out in the heavens until they touch each other. Thus the covering will be complete, and they will give spiritual shade to a whole nation, protecting it from demonic rule and evil spiritual assaults. Then we can expect times of unprecedented blessing upon Earth.

DAVID—ALLEGORY OF BUILDING THE CITY

We have already looked carefully at David and his kingdom as a powerful allegory of Jesus and how He will build His Church. The fortified city of Jerusalem, which God instructed David to build, is also a similar allegory that gives many insights as to how heavenly Jerusalem was built and how it functions.

During the last 30 years of King David's reign and in the early years of King Solomon's reign, we can see a true picture of how God wanted the Church to be built. Unfortunately, Solomon's kingdom fell into apostasy after a few years. This was mainly due to the death of David and the abandonment of David's tabernacle, with its pure and passionate worship. In addition, the corrupting influence of Solomon's pagan wives soon led him—and then many of the leaders and the people—into compromise, immorality, and the corrupting worship of other gods.

CITIES, NOT VILLAGES

As we have already seen in biblical times, only strong, fortified cities could exercise rule and government over the whole region and withstand invaders that came against them. A king could not rule a land without having control of a network of strong cities that established and upheld his rule.

No one seeking to conquer a land could succeed as long as the cities of that land were not taken and under his command. In terms of rule and government, whoever had control of the cities had control of the land, and whoever lost control of the cities lost control of the land.

The villages were powerless in this matter. They could not of themselves rule over anything, and they automatically suffered the consequences of whatever happened to the cities. From the villages it was possible to carry out some forms of guerrilla warfare and harass the enemy king who ruled from the cities to some extent. But to wrest the rule and government and take control, the cities themselves had to be taken.

I began to see that this very important principle explained to me why, in spite of the great growth of the Charismatic Movement in the 1960s, the enemy continued to hold such sway in our society and clearly still ruled in our cities and over the society's major institutions. We had been building many individual, autonomous local churches, which were like isolated villages. They were *not* city churches.

In Old Testament times, the villages relied on the cities for their provisions, government, and protection. They lived in the shadow of the cities and paid tribute to them. Every strong city had a large number of satellite villages over which they exercised authority.

RESTORATION IN THE SCRIPTURES

God's nation, comprised of Jews, was intended to be His glory and His government in the earth. When Israel finally entered the Promised Land, they began well enough. But they soon tired in their zeal to possess their inheritance, and they sinned persistently against God. They were finally judged and sent into captivity. Even in their judgment, God promised them that it would only be for a limited period of 70 years; afterward He would restore them and rebuild the temple and the city (see Jer. 25:12; Isa. 44:24–45:13).

As we have already discussed in Chapter 1 of this book, these Scriptures were fulfilled through the prayers of Daniel, but also through the edicts of Cyrus, Darius, and Artaxerxes. Through Daniel, these three pagan kings came to fear the true God, but probably never came to really know Him. Within God's nation, the leadership of Zerubbabel, who rebuilt the temple, was an allegorical picture of the Church-building apostle. Joshua, the high priest, and Ezra, the teacher, also played a vital role.

A large section of the Old Testament covers this period of history. Once again, these Scriptures are not included in our Bibles just to teach us some interesting Jewish history. They are powerful allegories of Jesus and His Kingdom; they are written for our instruction and especially for those on whom the end of the age has come. The main purpose of these biblical books of restoration is to teach principles by which God will bring about a glorious restoration of His Church at the end of the age.

All the prophetic Scriptures from Isaiah to Malachi focus on this short period of history—about 150 years. At the same time, they are speaking of and looking forward to the great events of restoration, which are promised at the end of the age, to prepare the way for the return of Jesus.

Six books of the Old Testament are devoted entirely to the actual years of restoration and teach us many important principles concerning restoration in the Church. These books are Ezra, Nehemiah, Esther, Haggai, Zechariah, and Malachi.

During their captivity, the people of God continued to meet together in small synagogues. These buildings normally held 100 to 200 people and were scattered around the various countries of the Mediterranean. Here the Jews of the dispersion met to read the Scriptures, sing the psalms, and lament their condition as captives of Babylon (see Psalm 137).

This is such a picture of the recent history of the Church and of Judaism. Because of sin and disobedience, both have become captives of the "Babylonian" world system. Christians and Jews largely meet in small buildings in just the same way as the Jews did during their Babylonian captivity. Instead of being God's government on the earth, the Church constantly has to seek permission from her "Babylonian captors" (the world's political, legal, and civil authorities and economic systems) for everything she does.

In the days of Cyrus, when the call came to return and rebuild the ruined temple and the city of Jerusalem, only a minority of Jews responded. The majority were too comfortable in Babylon. However, some did set out in difficult circumstances, leaving their homes and synagogues behind, to rebuild the temple and the city. The story is recorded in Ezra and Nehemiah.

They were appalled and discouraged at the devastation they found and worked slowly and painfully to recover usable stones from the rubble that remained. With this makeshift building material, they started to rebuild the temple. As we have already read, they only got as far as the foundation level after four years. The builders were tempted and opposed on all sides as summarized below:

1. They were tempted to compromise and made unholy alliances
    with false friends who claimed they wanted to help. Some of
    these "friends" claimed to be close relatives serving the same
    God, but they were of a totally different heart and spirit.
    Warned by God's prophetic word, the true restoration people
    rightly refused to compromise with these false friends (see
    Ezra 4:1-4).

2. As time went on, they became exhausted and discouraged saying, "I never realized it was going to be this hard. We just don't seem to be getting anywhere, and the obstacles are too great. It's futile, let's just give up."

3. They opted for postponement due to the difficulties, saying; "It's the wrong time to build the house of the Lord. Let's wait for things to change and get easier."

4. They became distracted and turned to building more comfortable homes for themselves instead of trying to continue with building the temple of the Lord.

Four years after their return from Babylon, everything concerning the temple ceased and nothing more was done for another 14 years (see Ezra 4:24). Then two young Jewish prophets named Haggai and Zechariah came on the scene praying and prophesying. Haggai particularly brought some very specific words from God that spoke directly into that immediate situation. He prophesied five times in a three-and-a-half-month period. As a result, a new spirit from God came upon the leaders and the people, and they were stirred up to begin to work again on the temple. The circumstances hadn't changed, but their spirits were radically changed, and now nothing would stop them. Like Peter in Acts 4:18-20, they decided to obey God rather than submit any longer to the severe opposition from the local political leaders or the political oppression and unjust laws from Sushan, the capital city of the Persian-Median Empire.

Suddenly, through their praying and prophesying, the whole political situation radically changed back in their favor. The wicked king, Cambyses II, was assassinated. Another younger son of Cyrus called Darius II came to the throne in Sushan. Darius had his father's integrity and gentle character. He changed the law back to what it had been under his father, so as to allow the Jews to build the temple. He also gave generous political and financial support to the project. As a result, the temple was completed in 516 B.C., after just four years' work.

Twenty-two years had passed from when King Cyrus issued the first commandment to rebuild the temple in 538 B.C.

Now the Jews had a beautiful temple in which to worship. They reestablished all the pageantry, traditions, and ceremony of their ancient religion and restored the function of the Levitical priesthood. With the homes they had built for themselves and with their new temple, they were now much more comfortable in their family life and church life.

For many years after the temple was completed, nothing was done to restore the rest of Jerusalem, which remained in ruins with no wall or gates. The inhabitants would leave their beautiful homes where God was honored and go to the beautiful temple where God was worshiped. In between lay the ruined city of Jerusalem; no one had any heart or faith to believe that the city also could be restored. It continued this way for 71 years, from 516 B.C. to 445 B.C.

But God was preparing a man who was going to change everything and bring about the next stage of restoration, which was the rebuilding of the city. This story is told in the books of Ezra and Nehemiah. The opposition to building the temple had been severe, but God's builders learned not to compromise with the enemy or allow exhaustion or discouragement to rob them of their faith. They learned to avoid distractions and understood that, in God's eyes, quitting is not acceptable. No matter how difficult the work seems, God will make a way where there seems to be no way.

God's people were soon to discover that the resistance to building the city was going to be even greater than the opposition they experienced while rebuilding the temple. We'll examine the lessons of this in the next chapter.

ENDNOTES

1. Biblesoft's New Exhaustive Strong's Numbers and Concordance with Expanded Greek-Hebrew Dictionary. CD-ROM. Biblesoft, Inc.

and International Bible Translators, Inc. (© 1994, 2003, 2006), s.v. "Endunamoo," (NT 1743).

2. Ibid., s.v. "Dunamis," (NT 1411).

3. William Blake, "Jerusalem," *PoetryArchive.com,* http://www.poetry-archive.com/b/jerusalem.html (accessed June 11, 2011).

CHAPTER 8

THE ORDER OF
REBUILDING THE CITY

THE enemy often sees the way God is moving before His own people do. Satan then begins to fight furiously to stop God's purposes being fulfilled even before God's people understand the implications of what God has already begun to do amongst them (see Ezra 4:1-5,13,16;19-20).

THE CRUCIAL ROLE OF NEHEMIAH

In the capital city of Sushan was a young Jewish man of great ability called Nehemiah. He had worked himself up to a position of great trust alongside Artaxerxes, the ruler of the Persian-Median Empire. Nehemiah was now the personal assistant, or cupbearer, to Artaxerxes, who literally trusted Nehemiah with his life.

The Book of Nehemiah begins with the story of how some brethren had just come to visit Nehemiah from Jerusalem. They came with a heartbreaking report of the distressing condition of the Jews who were now living in the burned and ruined city. This caused Nehemiah to weep bitterly with fasting and prayer for the city of his fathers. He cried out to God in deep repentance for the way they had acted so corruptly in not keeping His commandments. He reminded God of His promise that even after He had scattered them, He would return them to the place which He had chosen as a dwelling place for His name—if they would return to Him and keep His commandments (see Neh. 1:4-11). It is important for us to remember that it is OK to remind God of what He has promised us.

Nehemiah then came before the king with a very sad face because of his breaking heart. He was compelled by the king to reveal what was troubling him. He told the king of his agony and pain over the condition of the city of Jerusalem, "the city and place of his fathers' tombs" (see Neh. 2:3). Nehemiah asked to be allowed to go back to Jerusalem, and declared by dogged God-given faith that, if he were permitted to go back there, he would rebuild the city.

Amazingly, King Artaxerxes released Nehemiah to go and rebuild the city. The king also released all the timber, raw materials, and money Nehemiah would need for the reconstruction. He then appointed Nehemiah as governor over the city and over the region and gave him letters of authority to all the nearby governors (see Neh. 2:2-8).

Nehemiah, now the city governor appointed and sent by Artaxerxes, was a great allegorical picture of a city-building apostle whose role was absolutely crucial.

We must note the difference between the apostolic ministries of Zerubbabel and Nehemiah: Zerubbabel was an allegorical type of a church-building apostle; Nehemiah was an allegorical type of a city-building apostle. Both were necessary and had to work together in their different spheres to see complete restoration of society.

Nehemiah was served by many other wonderful leaders who worked under his inspiration and leadership. Most of those leaders had already been in the city for years. However, until Nehemiah came on the scene with the necessary authority and resources, there was no one able to pull everyone together and get them working as a team on the one master plan to bring restoration.

STEPS TO REBUILDING THE RUINED CITY

God found in Nehemiah the character and qualities that He could use to restore Jerusalem. *Selecting the right leader was the first step in rebuilding the city.*

Nehemiah was a man burdened and heartbroken for the city of his forefathers and for the people living in such dire conditions. He wept and mourned over it for many days.

He was a humble man of prayer and sacrifice as he fasted and sought the Lord day and night for as long as it took to get an answer. He gave God honor as he prayed and repented for his sins and the sins of his people. He prayed reminding God of the Word given to Moses for His people: He said that He would gather those who had been scattered and, if they returned and kept His commandments, He would return them to His dwelling place (see Neh. 1:4-11).

When the king asked why he was sad, Nehemiah prayed to the Lord for the right answer to give. It took great boldness to ask the king as the Lord instructed, but because of Nehemiah's obedience, he was released to leave Shushan—and he was given everything that was needed to complete the rebuilding of Jerusalem.

Nehemiah was a man willing to pay the price. From a good comfortable job in the king's palace in Sushan, where he had great favor, he went to live in the ruins of Jerusalem, where he was put under great pressure to keep the peace with surrounding governors.

He was a man of faith who declared to Artaxerxes that, "with your permission, I will rebuild it" (see Neh. 2:5). Nehemiah believed God could use him to do it. He understood the difficulty of his task. The extent of the difficulty can be seen in that he asked the king for letters to the governors and keeper of the forest, a house in which to live, and captains with soldiers to protect him.

The second step in rebuilding the city was when Nehemiah got the plan from God and acted on it, setting a time for completion and then working to that end to accomplish his God-given purpose. He was a man willing to act. He was a doer, not just a dreamer or even just a "pray-er." Realizing that rebuilding a ruined city would take hard work over a long period of time, he took a careful survey and was totally realistic about what he was taking on.

Nehemiah was just a man who feared the king; he understood the risk he took when his sadness was uncovered in the king's presence and surely had moments of feeling totally inadequate. Although he did not move in fleshly self-confidence, he was prepared to stick like glue to the word God had given him; he did not let fear or his sense of inadequacy paralyze him!

The third step in rebuilding the city was applying his leadership and administrative skills to carry out God's plan. Nehemiah was able to lead, direct, organize, and bring unity among many different leaders. Each was building their own part in their own way in their own locality. He was not an autocratic controller, yet he acted with real authority as he facilitated, directed, and coordinated others to work together in unity.

The workers consisted of businessmen, politicians, judges, priests, and ordinary folk of various trades and tribes. But they all got together and began working under Nehemiah's leadership. Each one built in front of his own house (within his own sphere of influence). But it was one wall, and through Nehemiah's leadership, God made it all fit together.

Nehemiah was able to enlist secular, political, and financial support from kings and leaders who liked him and trusted him. He was not a "flake" or a weird person in the eyes of the secular world. The support and help of these influential secular leaders was a vital part of fulfilling the sovereign purposes of God. But there were some who opposed him. So it was still a battle for every inch of the wall. Active political opposition had hindered the purposes of God and stopped the work for 14 years. However, Nehemiah was prepared to persevere until it was finished.

Nehemiah was a man who would not let fear hinder him and who could not be intimidated. He did not allow his natural apprehension to stop him from fulfilling God's purpose. He feared God much more than he feared people.

The fourth step in rebuilding the city was taking action to defend the builders on the wall. Nehemiah was a builder and a warrior, knowing how to defend himself and those with him. He set a watch, day and night, against all attacks.

The workers worked with their trowels in one hand and their swords at the ready, to be used when needed. Always ready to stand up to the opposition, each man used one hand to build and one hand to fight and defend against all attacks. There was no dichotomy or separation between secular and spiritual, or church and state. A builder who could not wage war or a warrior who could not build was of no use in this situation. Everyone had to have both skills. Because they were all armed and dangerous and ready to fight, the attack never came.

THE ROLE OF EZRA

A great prophetic intercessor named Ezra had arrived in the city in 458 B.C., which was 13 years before Nehemiah returned. Ezra was an able teacher, had a great prayer life, and carried the same heart and burden for the city. But he did not have the gift to lead and mobilize the builders or warriors the way that Nehemiah did. (Remember also, that many of the leaders who were drawn to Nehemiah were secular businessmen and political leaders.)

Ezra did not have the apostolic gift and leadership anointing of Nehemiah, but he prayed desperately for the city. The temple had been rebuilt and was in daily use. Nehemiah then arrived in the city and organized all the leaders; they set to work, and in 52 days the wall was rebuilt. Then God used the prophetic teaching gift of Ezra to bring deep repentance to the people that resulted in a powerful revival.

It was Ezra, not Nehemiah, who was the instrument God used for spiritual revival in the city (see Neh. 8–10). But Nehemiah was the one God used to set it all up apostolically! Each had a unique, individual role to play. There was no competition, and abundant grace was upon them all. They were a non-competitive team working together under Nehemiah's leadership.

THE BATTLE FOR THE WALLS

When the people began to build the walls according to Nehemiah's plan, there was immediate, tremendous opposition. The enemies of the Jews knew that if the walls were completed and the gates were hung, the city would become secure and the rule of the whole land of Israel from Jerusalem would begin soon afterward. Every means was used by their enemies to try to stop this from happening.

Despite this, Nehemiah pressed on and urged all the leaders to be ready to fight as well as to build. If the enemy attacked at any particular point along the wall, the ones nearest that area were commanded to blow a trumpet and call for help. Then they would all come together to that place and support their brethren to resist the attack. (See Nehemiah 4:17-20.) No one could work in isolation and concentrate only on his own thing at his particular part of the wall. They had to work together as one team, although they were spread out in many places all around the wall.

Nehemiah said to them:

> *Do not be afraid of them. Remember the Lord, great and awesome, and fight for your brethren, your sons, your daughters, your wives, and your houses* (Nehemiah 4:14).

Under Nehemiah, each builder restored the part of the wall that was in front of his own house. Each man built a house of his own in his own particular style. But each also took responsibility for the part of the wall that was adjacent to his own house within the city. The builders worked in such a way that what they were doing fitted into the overall plan and formed a continuous wall without any breaks. There was unity, order, and relationship in what they were doing. They recognized Nehemiah's overall governmental headship of the city and adhered to the single city plan of which they were all part.

Nehemiah, the governor of the city, with the many other leaders working with him, accomplished *the fifth step in rebuilding the city by completing the wall in an amazing 52 days!* The city was now well on the way to being made secure. But the gates also had to be established. (The whole story is told in Nehemiah 3:1–6:19.)

Once the wall was finished, they continued rebuilding the city as a united team under the governor. There were many leaders working together and many individual projects with different responsibilities and specific roles for each person.

The completion of this wall meant a new security and protection for all those who lived in the city. It now had definite boundaries and clearly-defined city limits. As a result, each person had to decide whether to live inside or outside the walls. Those who lived inside were more secure, but had to come under the authority and government of the elders of the city who ruled over them from the nearest gate.

The sixth step in rebuilding the city was the hanging of doors on the gates of the city. Nehemiah's builders did this by hanging strong metal-reinforced wooden doors at each end of the entrance tunnels, which had been deliberately made through the wall at intervals around the whole perimeter. This allowed people, carriages, and merchandise to enter and leave the city at a number of different points. It was these tunnels, plus the doors, which were called the Gates of the City. The tunnels were quite long, as the city walls of those ancient cities could be up to 100 feet thick. The doors at each end were closed at night to protect the city so it could be kept absolutely secure through the hours of darkness.

ELDERS RULED IN THE GATES

At each gate, a group of elders was appointed. They sat on thrones at the gates with armed guards available to them. From this position they could observe everyone who passed into and out of the city. They could examine the contents of any wagon to see what it contained and then decide whether to let the people and their merchandise in. They could also prevent anyone leaving in an unlawful manner. At least one of the elders from each gate also sat with the governor on the city council and helped govern the entire city.

In addition, the people who lived near a particular gate would come to the elders at that gate to have their disputes settled. So the elders also acted like local judges or magistrates.

We see a great allegorical example of this in the Book of Ruth when Boaz went to elders in the gate to settle the inheritance issue with his near relative. It had to be legally decided as to which of them would exercise their right of redemption as Naomi's closest relative after she and Ruth returned to Bethlehem from Moab. The nearest relative who had first claim to redemption stated before the elders that he did not want to exercise his right to redeem the land of Elimelech and marry Ruth. (See Ruth 4.)

All this was legally settled at the gate before the elders. Then Boaz, as the next nearest relative, was free to become the redeemer and buy back the land and marry Ruth. As a result, Ruth was now free to marry Boaz and recover all the lost inheritance of her former husband, one of two sons of Elimelech. She also bore children to Boaz and became the mother of Obed, the grandmother of Jesse and the great-grandmother of David. Thus, she became part of the direct bloodline of Jesus after the flesh. This is all a glorious allegorical picture of Christ and His Church. (See Ruth 4:13-17.)

In this way, city government was established. The city counselors ruled on behalf of the king under the direction of the governor, who planned a strategy to maintain the king's rule over the whole region. From there they subdued the region and ruled over it on behalf of the king. The local elders in the various gates ruled the daily lives of the people under the city governor's headship. The entire city was protected from thieves, robbers, and every kind of villain, for they could no longer enter freely at any point as they had before.

WATCHMEN ON THE WALLS

Lookouts were manned to watch day and night from the towers built into the walls so as to give early warning of anyone suspicious approaching the city. If it appeared dangerous, the guards were warned to mobilize and, if necessary, shut the gates of the city and be ready to resist any attack. Several examples of this are found in the Scriptures. In spiritual terms, these lookouts could be the prophetic intercessors who could mobilize the spiritual warriors in a similar way.

Each city had an army garrison of seasoned warriors stationed within the city in order to enforce the king's rule over the land. They worked in and around the city to patrol the land and maintain the king's authority.

LIVING OUTSIDE THE CITY

As was mentioned earlier, some people preferred to live outside the city walls. They enjoyed some of the benefits of the city without being subject to its government or committed to its corporate life. But they were always the first casualties whenever an enemy attacked without warning! Villages were not able to provide what the stronger cities could because they were fewer in number, more vulnerable outside the protection of strong city walls, and had more limited resources with which to train warriors and resist invaders. In ancient times most of the farmers and workers lived within the city walls and went out into the fields during the day to work. When danger was imminent, the watchers on the wall blew trumpets to warn the people to come back inside the walls where they could be protected.

A PATTERN FOR THE CHURCH

All the principles of city government and city life discussed above are applicable to the Church. The city church is the fulfillment of all the types and shadows that are so powerfully illustrated here, including: the proper author-ity and power of the King; delegated leadership and an organized structure to do the work effectively; watchful lookouts in the form of intercessors to warn of danger; the necessary number of trained warriors to fight the battles and protect the leaders and the sheep; and the corporate resources to provide for the needs of the entire church. The city church can provide resources, training, and protection to the local churches until they grow strong enough to sustain themselves.

CHAPTER 9

JERUSALEM—THE FIRST CITY CHURCH

ON the Day of Pentecost, the first City Church was born, and it began to function as the first manifestation of the spiritual Heavenly Jerusalem. Within about two years, the Church in Jerusalem had the structure and numbers of a spiritual city

Extra-biblical records by reliable historians like Josephus, plus the writings of some early church fathers, such as Polycarp, and reliable Roman secular records estimate that within two years the Church had grown to about 20,000 members, which was about one-third of the city's population.

Through the mighty "one accord" prayer meeting in the upper room and the revelatory teaching of the Spirit of God, the newly-born Church emerged with great power and authority, demolishing the spiritual strongholds over the physical city of Jerusalem. This was immediately evidenced by the great harvest of 3,000 souls when Peter preached his first sermon (see Acts 2:14-41).

This first successful City Church in Jerusalem plus the other biblical examples of Antioch, Thessalonica, and Ephesus teach us many important principles regarding the establishing of spiritual cities today.

My understanding of this subject developed gradually over the years as a matter of practical necessity. During the last few decades of the 20th century, Eileen and I were privileged to visit many nations and carefully observe the big, new churches that were springing up in many places such as Seoul, Korea; the U.S.A.; various parts of Central and South America; and Africa (particularly, at that time, in South Africa).

I appreciated many powerful and good things about these churches, but I also observed that some of them had certain lacks. Vast crowds attended the meetings but, in some cases, proper government and essential pastoral care had not been established. The people came and went as they pleased without being properly committed or cared for. In most cases, the people were just part of a large, anonymous crowd. They attended meetings and were blessed by the glory that filled the atmosphere and by the amazing worship and music and the excellence of the ministry. But, as individuals, most of them had little influence inside the church; likewise, most were having no effect on the world outside the church.

Some of these churches also lacked the caring intimacy and the training to bring individual believers to maturity. After years of church attendance, they had many needs and were often still being harassed by the devil. We observed that the careful discipleship training capable of bringing individual believers to mature, victorious living and spiritual fruitfulness was best accomplished in house groups and smaller congregational meetings.

Some of these great churches, such as the one led by Dr. David Yonggi Cho in Seoul, Korea, had introduced all of the three levels of church life, namely: evangelizing home groups, congregational meetings, and large celebration meetings. In addition, there was considerable attention to teaching the people how to develop powerful, continuous prayer lives. Because of this, they were much more successful in retaining the harvest and bringing the believers to maturity.

SMALL IS BEAUTIFUL, BUT LESS POWERFUL

In our own situation in Watford, England, after we returned from India in 1976, we planted several churches. As they grew, we divided them into local, autonomous congregations of about 200 to 300 members. This was to minimize traveling and enable them to reach their local communities more effectively. With the division of the congregations, we soon discovered that we gained in close relationships amongst the people, but lost out in terms of power and impact upon our entire region.

A second problem was my own limited understanding, at that time, of the true biblical structure of the Church. I had been deeply impacted by the teaching of Watchman Nee and had embraced much of his teaching regarding who we are in Christ (as described in his first book, *The Normal Christian Life*). I was also strongly impacted by the kind of church structure that was described in his second book, *The Normal Christian Church Life*. I had always believed strongly in the local, autonomous church and felt it should be free from the external denominational control of some remote headquarters that might even be located in another state or nation.

Yet in our leadership meetings, we were feeling more and more strongly that the Lord was leading us to create one church of several congregations in our region with one apostolic government over them all. Our problem at that time was to explain how we could justify a special relationship between the five congregations that we had become. After already establishing them as five self-governing, autonomous churches, how could we legitimately go back to one government over all five?

Undoubtedly, giving absolute local autonomy, authority, and independence to each church had diluted the excellence, weakened the thrust, and reduced the former growth. As the revelation of the city church became clearer to me, we began to see that we needed to rethink our organizational structure.

It was a great joy for me to discover that about ten years after Watchman Nee had written *The Normal Christian Church Life,* he spoke again to his leaders on this subject and confessed to some of the problems his previous methods had caused. These messages were translated and printed in another, not so well-known, book under the title, *Further Talks on Church Life*. In this book, Watchman Nee stated that he had failed to recognize the special function of certain churches like Jerusalem and Antioch, which were clearly "regional centers" and not ordinary local churches. These churches had formed a regional residential base for apostles, prophets, and other Ephesians 4:11 ministries and were regional in their authority and influence, as well as increasingly worldwide in their impact.

I then began to see that God had called us to be such a regional or city church. Our regional responsibility was for the three nearby towns of Hemel Hempstead, St. Albans, and Watford, plus all the other smaller villages and towns in between them. A 15-mile diameter circle roughly enclosed all of these towns and villages, which had an aggregate population of approximately 300,000 at the time. We saw clearly that we were to create one city church made up of five related congregations with a plan to plant many more related congregations within this circle. Thus, we reorganized ourselves to become a regional/city church made up of several local churches, each with their own local elders, but all under one Ephesians 4:11 city church government led by a plurality of apostles and prophets.

ZECHARIAH'S VISION

In Zechariah 1:14-21 we read:

> *So the angel who spoke with me said to me, "Proclaim, saying, 'Thus says the LORD of hosts: "I am zealous for Jerusalem and for Zion with great zeal. I am exceedingly angry with the nations at ease; for I was a little angry, and they helped—but with evil intent." Therefore thus says the LORD: "I am returning to Jerusalem with mercy; My house shall be built in it," says the LORD of hosts, "And a surveyor's line shall be stretched out over Jerusalem."' "Again proclaim, saying, 'Thus says the LORD of*

*hosts:"My cities shall again spread out through prosperity; the L*ORD *will again comfort Zion, and will again choose Jerusalem."""*

*Then I raised my eyes and looked, and there were four horns. And I said to the angel who talked with me, "What are these?" So he answered me, "These are the horns that have scattered Judah, Israel, and Jerusalem." Then the L*ORD *showed me four craftsmen. And I said, "What are these coming to do?" So he said, "These are the horns that scattered Judah, so that no one could lift up his head; but the craftsmen are coming to terrify them, to cast out the horns of the nations that lifted up their horn against the land of Judah to scatter it."*

When the Jews returned to rebuild the city in 538 B.C., they had first concentrated on building the temple. As we have already seen, while it was still at the foundation level, they lost heart to continue, and everything remained on hold for 14 years.

At this point, Haggai prophesied and galvanized the dispirited Jews to start the work again. At the same time, Zechariah also began to prophesy and, in classic prophetic style, was carried in the Spirit to see beyond the present, small, physical reality of the partly rebuilt temple to the great, end-time spiritual reality that this whole exercise allegorically represented.

Zechariah was taken by the angel and saw four horns (figuratively this Hebrew word for *horns* means "power" and is often used prophetically to symbolize power or authority).[1] Here it represents four mighty demonic powers ruling over the nations that had scattered the people of God *"so that no one could lift up his head"* (Zech. 1:21). Then Zechariah lifted up his eyes and saw four craftsmen. He learned that these craftsmen had come to terrorize these horns, destroy them, and cast them out of the nations.

The horns represented these four strong satanic powers that had been able to wreak havoc among God's people, the Jews, because they had not been obedient to Him. There was much discouragement among them because of the way that satan had been able to scatter them so effectively.

But in typical prophetic style, God was causing Zechariah to run his prophetic eyes down the centuries yet to come to see the far greater fulfillment at the end of the age involving the Church in all the nations of the earth.

In a similar way, these strong satanic "horns" have been at work in a fourfold attack to undermine the pillars of our society. This demonic attack started in earnest amongst the Western, traditionally Christian nations, as they entered into the 20th century. It was a progressive fourfold attack as follows:

The first phase was an attack upon God Himself as creator and sovereign ruler over all that He had made. This happened through embracing the so-called "age of reason" based upon the ancient philosophies of Greece, which taught that people were now progressing to become like God through the power of their own reason. This really takes us back to the first temptation by satan to entice Adam to step out from God-dependence into independence and become "like God" by developing his own intellectual resources.

The second phase was an attack upon God's Word and its infallibility. So-called "higher criticism" began to question even the trustworthiness of the translations as well as the original documents. This destroyed the foundation for faith; as a result, people were restricted to only *believe* what they could intellectually understand.

The third phase was to challenge all the laws of morality and righteousness upon which our society was based. These laws were derived from the Scriptures concerning marriage, family, sexual purity, covenant, honesty, and truth.

The fourth phase was to totally embrace a philosophy of evolution. This not only affected physical creation, but even our minds, the way we think, and views as to what is right and wrong. No longer would anything be seen as being eternally right or wrong, good or evil on the basis of God's say-so. Instead, everything was open to question and redefinition according to what seemed best to the individual at the time

In Zechariah's vision, God's answer to this terrible destructive work among His people was the raising up of the four craftsmen. They had the power to utterly rout demonic powers and cast them out of the nations.

We need to know prophetically who these craftsmen are. We need to understand what they did that was so terrifying and effective in destroying the demonic powers typified by the strong horns.

I believe we must understand this truth in order to defeat the powers of darkness that hold such sway in our land today.

EPHESIANS 4:11 GIFTS AND ZECHARIAH'S VISION

There is a connection between the Ephesians 4:11 gifts and the vision given to Zechariah. Before we make that connection, let's explore some views on the gifts named in Ephesians 4:11.

There has been a fair amount of debate over many years as to whether the ministries mentioned in Ephesians 4:11 are fivefold or fourfold. Some have suggested that the pastor and teacher are one in the same person; there is a slight hint in the Greek to possibly support this.

What I have begun to see is that both positions are actually right. There are only four different ministry skills, but they reside in five different kinds of leaders who function in what is usually called the Ephesians 4:11 ministries. Most often called the fivefold ministries, they are also known as the *ascension gift ministries*.

The four ministry skills are:

- Prophet
- Evangelist
- Pastor
- Teacher

The apostle is not just another ministry skill, but an anointed person with exceptional leadership skills and special wisdom from God to build the Kingdom on His unshakable foundation (see 1 Cor. 3:10). Apostles also have a unique ability to lead and put to work the other four ministry skills already mentioned.

When true apostles direct the activity of the ministry skills, they make each of them much more fruitful and effective. At least one of these ministry skills would always be resident in the apostle, but the apostle can draw on the skills in other men and women and put them to work as a team with the wisdom and leadership skills that are the mark of the true apostle.

In fact, I now believe that ideal, fully-formed, mature apostles have all these four ministry skills within themselves, just as Jesus and Paul did. This enables the apostle to empathize with all the different ministries, direct them, train them, and activate their gifts and callings more effectively because the apostle already has firsthand experience and is familiar with the practicalities of the work they are called to do.

If all these ministry skills do not reside within the apostle, it is even more essential that the apostle work in close relationship with other well-developed Ephesians 4:11 ministries who have the skill or skills the apostle lacks. This particularly applies to the biblical need for apostles to work in partnership with mature prophets. When these other ministries are joined to the apostle, they not only supply any missing skills; they also enable the apostle to fulfill the apostle's ministry.

The chief purpose of the apostle is to develop and direct the Ephesians 4:11 ministries in building the city church to be effective in the region and to the nations of the world as God directs. It is not enough to just give advice and counsel to pastors and elders on how to run better local churches.

Emerging present-day apostolic ministries really need to see the heavenly City of Jerusalem and understand that their call to build it is a first priority. When this happens, we shall see all that Zechariah saw in the Spirit being manifested in the Church today. In particular, we will see the releasing of "the four craftsmen" with the power to terrorize the demonic rulers who control this present darkness. We will then have the authority to cast them out of our nations. The means of achieving this is by building strong, fortified, "spiritual" cities that can wrest the rule of the heavens from the powers of darkness and establish the canopy of heavenly Jerusalem and the rule of the Kingdom of God over those earthly cities instead.

Immediately after seeing the craftsmen, Zechariah was shown the heavenly City of Jerusalem, for that was what these craftsmen were called to build. He then saw an angel with a measuring rod in his hand. The angel's job was to check the accuracy of the building. In every detail, it must be built to the exact pattern and dimensions set by God.

THE CITY ZECHARIAH SAW

Zechariah 2:1-5 reads:

> *Then I raised my eyes and looked, and behold, a man with a measuring line in his hand. So I said, "Where are you going?" And he said to me, "To measure Jerusalem, to see what is its width and what is its length." And there was the angel who talked with me, going out; and another angel was coming out to meet him, who said to him, "Run, speak to this young man, saying: 'Jerusalem shall be inhabited as towns without walls, because of the multitude of men and livestock in it. For I,' says the* LORD, *'will be a wall of fire all around her, and I will be the glory in her midst.'"*

DIAGRAM OF THE CITY CHURCH

Consider the following diagram in light of Zechariah's vision:

Apostles live in the glory with Ephesians 4 men and women, get their revelation there, and rule the city and the region for the King.

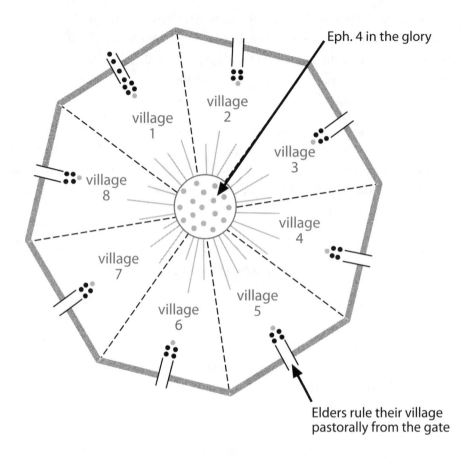

Eph. 4 in the glory

village 1

village 2

village 3

village 4

village 5

village 6

village 7

village 8

Elders rule their village
pastorally from the gate

What Zechariah saw when he lifted up his eyes was a city made up of a number of small towns or villages. They did not have walls separating them from one another because they were all dwelling together in unity. This caused a multitude of people to come together to form one great city with no divisions within it. The exterior of the whole city was surrounded by a wall of fire, not stone, and the *glory* of the Lord was in its midst.

In reality, at the time that Zechariah prophesied, he was looking at the physical foundations of the new temple that the Jews were rebuilding in the ruins of the destroyed city of Jerusalem. It was small and not very impressive compared with the temple that previously stood there. But in the Spirit, he was not seeing that physical temple at all. His prophetic eyes were looking down the centuries and seeing the heavenly reality that this temple allegorically represented.

Jesus, we are told, would build a spiritual temple made up of living stones, as described in several places in the New and the Old Testaments (see 1 Cor. 3:11-16; Eph. 2:19-22; 1 Pet. 2:4-10).

Zechariah was also seeing the heavenly city whose builder and maker was God, which God had first shown to Abraham (see Heb. 11:10). The glory Zechariah saw in the midst was the New Testament heavenly equivalent of David's tabernacle. This initially was the upper room in Jerusalem where the apostles, prophets, and Ephesians 4:11 ministries had come together with a small crowd of others to pray and worship and war and seek the face of God—just like David's mighty men had done in the past. There they received revelation, wisdom, and strategy for establishing the city, governing the Kingdom, and successfully waging spiritual warfare against their enemies.

Each village within the city represents a local church with all the qualities of local church life. But each village was also a segment of the city. There were no walls around any of the individual villages within the city, but there was one great impregnable wall of fire completely surrounding the whole city and protecting all that was in the city from demonic invasion.

Individually, the villages had all the benefits and intimacy of the family life of a local church, but corporately, with all the villages joined together, they had the power, visibility, and impact of a mighty city church!

ENDNOTE

1. *Strong's Exhaustive Concordance*, Hebrew #7161.

CHAPTER 10

OCCUPYING THE GATES
OF THE HEAVENLY CITY

IT is important to look further at what the gates of this city allegorically represent. The function of gates in natural governmental terms was explained earlier. This was powerfully illustrated in the days of David's kingdom and again in the restored city of Jerusalem when it was rebuilt in the days of Nehemiah.

THE GATES BECOME SPIRITUAL

When we come to the books of the prophets and to some other Old Testament Scriptures, we find these gates being spoken of prophetically; they are seen by the prophets to be spiritual, in the heavens, and not physical, on earth.

When we then go to the New Testament, we find these gates spoken of allegorically by Jesus in the same way. Let us now look at what these gates mean in terms of a strategy for establishing the Kingdom of God in our cities today.

The first thing that Jesus said about the Church He would build was that the *"gates of Hades shall not prevail against it"* (Matt. 16:18). These gates came to represent the demonic spiritual powers that ruled over the cities from the heavenly realm. Those powers, through their various human agencies, regulated all that was allowed to come into the city spiritually, and they also controlled what was permitted to take place legally and politically in the city. Today, in many nations, these spiritual powers control many of the pillars of our society and the secular laws to such a degree that these spirits now rule the lives of the people in our cities. As I write, most of these spiritual gates over our cities are occupied by demonic powers working through their human agencies and not by God's people.

Long ago, satan took control of these gates in order to dominate our cities for his purposes. His occupancy in most cases is almost total. From these spiritual gates in the heavenly places, the influence of hell is much greater than the influence of Heaven; this is true for the majority of our cities.

This is how Jerusalem was controlled during the days of Jesus' ministry on earth. Demonic powers, working through the religious and political leaders of the day such as the Sanhedrin, Herod, and Pilate, were able to significantly limit the ministry of Jesus and His impact upon the city. Jesus knew that until He rose triumphantly from the dead with all power and authority in Heaven and earth in His hands, these demonic powers could not be cast down. But once Jesus had risen and the Holy Spirit had fallen on the disciples on the Day of Pentecost, everything changed. The disciples quickly learned how to cast down these spirit powers over the city of Jerusalem.

Therefore, in order for the Kingdom to come to our cities in the same Pentecostal power of the first century Church, we must learn to retake these gates out of the enemy's hands and cast down these ruling spirits.

In Scripture, God has given us great promises concerning these gates. In Genesis 22, God spoke to Abraham after he had offered his only son, Isaac, saying:

> *Indeed I will greatly bless you, and I will greatly multiply your seed as the stars of the heavens, and as the sand which is on the seashore; and* **your seed shall possess the gate of their enemies.** *In your seed all the nations of the earth shall be blessed, because you have obeyed My voice* (Gen. 22:17-18 NASB).

God promised Abraham that the true descendants of Abraham would, by faith, possess the gates of their enemies, resulting in the reaping of a mighty harvest.

In Genesis 24 we have a beautiful allegory of Christ and His Church. Isaac is the bridegroom representing Christ, and Rebekah is the bride representing the Church. Rebekah's relatives are about to send her away to be married to Isaac. In verse 60 something is promised to the bride, Rebekah, and allegorically to the Church:

> *They blessed Rebekah and said to her:"Our sister, may you become the mother of thousands of ten thousands; **and may your descendants possess the gates of those who hate them"** (Gen. 24:60).*

The promise of reaping a mighty harvest is directly linked with taking possession of the gates that are presently in the hands of our enemy. Gate-taking was and still is a necessary preparation for city-taking. Also, once these gates are retaken, the spiritual blindness affecting the minds of many people will be immediately removed—and then the harvest can be reaped.

PHYSICAL GATES DIFFER FROM SPIRITUAL GATES

I do not believe it is enough to physically drive around a city and focus only on the major highways and other main entry points leading in and out of it. This can sometimes be the right thing to do, providing we have definitely heard from God and have some good spiritual reason for focusing in this way. But, we cannot make it an automatic methodology.

We must only do this when God has specifically shown us first that these locations are spiritual strongholds or gates "erected" through some present or historical situation, and second, that they need to be taken back.

The gates that Jesus and the prophets referred to were not that kind of physical gate. Rather, they were spheres of influence and control emanating from the heavens that shaped the way the people of the city thought and behaved. They also controlled many of the civil laws and judicial decisions that were made to govern them. For clarity, let me now divide these spiritual "gates" into three categories.

CATEGORY #1: GATES THAT CONTROL PEOPLE'S THINKING

These gates are largely responsible for shaping the worldview of most people. They influence people's minds and strongly formulate the way people think and behave. Several Scriptures tell us that we are fighting a battle for the minds of men, women, and especially children. The apostle Paul explains this truth in Second Corinthians 4:4:

> *Whose minds the god of this age has blinded, who do not believe, lest the light of the gospel of the glory of Christ, who is the image of God, should shine on them.*

Within this category of mind-influencing gates are several subcategories; let me define them as follows:

1) The Media

The media, including radio, television, movies, the Internet, iPods and other devices, DVDs, magazines, newspapers, and so forth, powerfully influence the way most people think. These gates largely shape worldviews.

2) The Education System

The present system of education is based in totally secular, humanistic, evolutionary philosophies that are often reinforced by atheistic or polytheistic worldviews. This system has, to a great extent, shaped the minds and perspectives of almost all of us from our earliest school days.

3) Various Religious Systems Making Significant Inroads in Our Cities

Ancient pagan religions, such as those practiced by Aztecs and druids, and including Hinduism, Buddhism, Confucianism, and the more recent religion of Islam, are resurging. These belief systems are now being widely taught, practiced, and tolerated in the United States and throughout the world. In addition, many of the traditional Christian denominations have fallen away and developed religious systems that are far removed from God and the truths of Scripture and are syncretistic and humanistic in their teaching and philosophy. There are also a number of more recent cults, some of which claim to be "Christian," but are teaching false doctrines; others are unashamedly pagan, occult, and anti-Christian.

4) The Political System and Institutions of Government

If you read any honest history book about the United States, it is obvious that the majority of the founding fathers of the United States of America were God-fearing men with high standards of integrity and morality. Most of them were bold Christians who were also men of prayer. They openly prayed, individually and corporately, for God's wisdom for the Constitution they were writing and the political structure they were forming. The Constitution was written based on these values.

These men, and often their families, came largely from European nations controlled by corrupt religious systems that worked in partnership with equally corrupt political systems. Together, these systems dominated the lives of ordinary people and exploited them financially and in every other way. Therefore, our Founding Fathers were determined to maintain freedom from any such system in America's newly-formed government.

This resulted in the now famous First Amendment, which prohibited the making of any law respecting the establishment of religion. This has been interpreted by some as a "separation of church and state," although those words were never actually used in the Constitution. The Founding Fathers never intended there to be any separation between the one true God and the State. Nor was there any confusion as to who that God was. To them, He was the God and Father of our Lord Jesus Christ.

If we were to turn our attention to other nations of the world, we would have to write another whole book to document the widespread corruption, greed, and lack of standards of honesty, integrity, or morality in almost every present political system ruling those nations. There are one or two exceptions, but of the present 192-member nations of the United Nations, you could probably count on the fingers of one hand the few truly upright moral leaders and governments of the nations having any integrity.

5) The Legal System and Institutions of Law

The original standards of integrity and impartiality for the federal and local judges of the United States, including even the Supreme Court, have been seriously eroded in recent years. Most judges unashamedly exhibit a strong political or moral bias in the judgments they bring. In addition, generally speaking, the attorneys who plead in these courts are not really concerned that justice should be done, but that they may win their case by any "legal" means so as to make money for themselves and for their clients.

6) Financial Institutions and Financial Systems

In recent months to our horror, most of us have discovered the depths of depravity operating in those people and financial institutions whose integrity we trusted. These "pillars" of our society and our economy have suddenly been exposed, and some have collapsed in ruins. As a result, millions of workers and other innocent victims have lost their means of livelihood.

The shock waves of this debacle have reverberated around the world to affect almost every nation. Our own economy in the U.S. has been shaken to the core. Political leaders and economic experts rush around, trying to salvage what they can and fix the enormous problems confronting us. The most disturbing feature of all this is that no one seems to be facing the real issue that caused of all this to happen, namely the insatiable greed and moral corruption in those who led these institutions. Until there is real repentance over these issues and a return to God-fearing righteousness, we will not find any *real* solutions.

John Wesley lived in similar times during which terrible moral corruption was exposed in government, banking, and official religious circles. The greatest investment scandal in history called The South Sea Bubble had just burst and devastated the economy of Britain and had seriously affected the United States and a number of other nations.

John Wesley frequently spoke a famous maxim in that time of spiritual revival in Great Britain: "Having, first, gained all you can and, secondly saved all you can, then give all you can!"[1] His words produced a tremendously positive surge in the economy that particularly benefited the lower-paid workers, many of whom had formerly been unemployed. His maxim needs to be rediscovered and practiced by everyone today.

7) Cultural Traditions of the City and the Nation

Some national cultures are so invaded by demonic powers that the norms of acceptable social behavior bear down heavily on all of society. Many true Christians buckle under the strain and live compromised lives in that stifling atmosphere. Once again, we see the same pressures affecting the way we live—and we must not give in to them.

The issues of speaking the truth, keeping our word, fulfilling our promises, paying our taxes honestly, and living as law-abiding citizens in all respects are mentioned many times in the Scriptures by Paul, Peter, and James.

These words of Scripture were written to Christians living in a pagan Roman society for which such godly cultural norms were nonexistent. Roman culture was also a very chauvinistic society with a low regard for women. Yet, from the beginning, the Church lived God's way and not according to pagan Roman culture. In a short time they began changing their society for the better. We see ungodly norms in a number of cultures today. We must not yield to them, even if we originate from one of those cultures.

We have much work to do. As you look at this list, tell me honestly from your own observation in this present time: How many of these "gates" are strongly influenced by the devil, and how many are powerfully influenced by the clear proclamation of the Kingdom of God by the true Church? I'm sure you would agree that in most cases these gates are almost totally in the control of the evil one. This tells us who is really running our cities and controlling our societies. It's time to change things; God is sending His Holy Spirit and empowering us to do just that!

This is a battle for the minds of people. As we read earlier, the Bible says that, *"the god of this world has blinded the minds of the unbelieving…"* (2 Cor. 4:4 NASB).

But it also tells us that *"it is the God who commanded light to shine out of darkness, who has shone in our hearts to give the light of the knowledge of the glory of God in the face of Jesus Christ"* (2 Cor. 4:6). He has also given us mighty and powerful weapons that are able to destroy everything that exalts itself against the knowledge of God (see 2 Cor. 10:4-5).

This is a fight that requires greater passion to win.

How much of what our children are learning in secular public schools makes them run after Jesus? How much do they learn that makes them run after the world and devilish things? How would you rate our universities in their desire or ability to lead students to seek after God? How about the media? If you're thinking like I am, you're saying, "Man, we have some work to do around here!"

We *must* take back the gates! The first way they can be taken is by praying for the people who already hold positions of great influence in these various realms. We must pray that they might be converted, or at least that their hearts are turned toward the Lord with a new godly fear.

There is no evidence that Nebuchadnezzar or Cyrus or Darius II were ever truly converted, but their hearts were definitely turned to have a healthy fear of the Lord God of Israel and a great respect for those who served Him. If they had been clearly and truly converted, that would have been even better. But even so, they were moved by the prayers of God's intercessors to serve the Lord's purposes and cause His will to be done on earth.

The second way to take these gates is for Christians to actually occupy these places and positions and become God's salt in that situation. They must be unashamed and courageous, yet wise witnesses who are powerful in prayer. It is no good gaining such a position and just being there quietly and secretly saying nothing and hoping to have some indirect influence.

Look at how Joseph always boldly and publicly recognized his God as the source of the great wisdom he exhibited. As an open worshiper of Jehovah, he was appointed to a political position second only to Pharaoh in the whole Egyptian Empire.

Also, look at the way Daniel behaved. He was in a secular government position all his life. He was a powerful political figure, second only to the various pagan kings whom he served. But he made it clear to each one of them that his prophetic wisdom and insight came directly from the God who was Jehovah, the God of the Jews, the only true God.

Neither of these men would be quiet about the Person and the Power who enabled them to be who they were and do what they did. They made it very clear that what they did with such wisdom and authority happened only because of the awesome God they served. At the risk of their lives, they would not keep quiet about their God. Nor would they lower their moral and ethical standards to keep out of trouble. Instead, they were able to change their secular demonic environments so that God was honored, revered, and finally obeyed. They changed the entire political atmosphere of nations.

We need to pray for Christians in these high positions in our nations so that they may have the same boldness, take the same uncompromising stand, and have the same influence on all they serve or rule over.

CATEGORY #2: GATES WHERE DEMONS ARE VENERATED AND WORSHIPED.

These are geographical sites of intense demonic strength and activity, such as temples, grottos, historic monuments, and worship sites where so-called "holy" objects, idols, and false gods were or still are being actively worshiped.

This includes shrines devoted to pagan gods or spirits, as well as places where statues of Mary, the Black Madonna, Baby Jesus, other "saints," or holy relics are venerated. It includes all the idols and religious objects of apostate Christianity and all the buildings, historic sites, and monuments of other religions and their false gods.

These gates would further include sites of witchcraft, especially places where witches, wizards, and warlocks gather, and shrines of demonic worship, especially places of present or past blood sacrifice, particularly human blood sacrifice.

In addition, sites where blood has been violently spilled, such as battle and massacre sites (particularly where vengeance was the motive of the massacre) can be powerful demonic gates. Other gates and areas include sites of sexual immorality, such as brothels or sex shops, and murder sites, such as abortion clinics.

These gates can only be taken by experienced, strong intercessors who know what they are doing and are truly being led by the Lord. It is usually necessary to go physically to those sites several times, sometimes over a prolonged period of time. In these situations, prayers that are Spirit-led and targeted by revelation of the Word must earnestly continue for a period of time. Sometimes praying right through the night as God directs is particularly effective. This is partly because so much demonic activity and witchcraft goes on under the cover of darkness.

God may direct the prayer team to perform certain specific prophetic acts. Prayers must be spoken in faith when and as God commands so as to tell the demons to leave, just as John did in the temple of Diana in Ephesus.[2]

Then they will have to obey. It's not how much noise you make, but the faith and authority by which you speak. All this must be done, not as a learned methodology, but only as God specifically directs and empowers His saints in a unique way in that particular situation and in His timing. Paul encountered Diana in Ephesus, but he didn't go into the temple or address her directly because the Lord did not give him that assignment. Intercessors *must* hear clearly from the Lord and *know* His timing when addressing these demonically controlled gates.

Once such a site has been cleansed, wherever possible, it needs to be permanently taken over by the saints and turned into a holy place of God's presence and peace.

Sometimes we have to learn how to go to such places in the Spirit because going there physically is impossible. It may be a private site within a city where we are not permitted to go, or it may be a closed country where Christians are not permitted. But, there are no barriers in the spirit realm, and God is beginning to teach us how to move and go in the Spirit to places where we cannot go openly and physically. This all has to be done as God specifically directs.

CATEGORY #3: GATES IN INDIVIDUALS POSSESSED BY MAJOR DEMONIC PRINCIPALITIES

These instances involve people who have deliberately given themselves to serve satan directly because of the power, prominence, and material benefits they obtain from him. But there is always a price that they have to pay. Satan is a hard taskmaster, even to his own.

When a major demonic principality has entered and now controls a person, it works through that person to control many other people. Sometimes one spirit in one person can strongly influence the behavior of hundreds of thousands of people throughout a whole nation or even several nations. In this way, these spirits are able to affect great portions of the earth. Recent historical and political examples would be Napoleon, Adolph Hitler, Joseph Stalin, Mussolini, or General Franco. A present-day religious example would be the Dalai Lama and the tens of thousands who attend his Mandala-making ceremonies in various locations as he travels worldwide.

There are others we could name who are presently active in various parts of the world today, including some within the United States. We must not be ignorant of these forces at work to control cities, regions, and the world. Some people are caught up in giving themselves passionately to what appears to be a great cause and don't realize the demonic impartation that accompanies their interaction.

A great biblical example of this kind of person was the zealous, fanatical, demonized Pharisee called Saul. Before his conversion, he rampaged through three nations persecuting and killing Christians, throwing many into prison, and inspiring many thousands of Jews to hate Christians, attack them, and even kill them. The spirit in this one man powerfully influenced thousands of people in three nations to behave like him and viciously persecute untold numbers of believers, even to death.

This human, demonically controlled gate was known by the first apostles. They stayed together in prayer in Jerusalem and refused to leave or be separated at the height of the persecution. Although the Scriptures do not actually record why the apostles stayed together, I believe from my own experience that the Spirit of God called the apostles to an emergency, powerful upper room prayer meeting to take this "gate" known as Saul. They prayed for the demon to be cast out of him. These prayers, plus the earlier dying prayers of Jesus and Stephen as Saul actively participated in each of their deaths, pricked his conscience deeply (see Luke 23:34; Acts 7:60).

As a result, Saul was suddenly and dramatically converted when he had a supernatural encounter with the risen Lord Jesus on the road to Damascus (see Acts 9). He was saved, delivered, and turned around on the spot to become one of the mightiest apostles of the early Church.

When this one man was converted and that gate was taken, the demonic activity of thousands of people which in turn had caused the persecution of many Christians suddenly ceased. The Christian Church in the three regions of Judea, Galilee, and Samaria suddenly had rest and were comforted, and the believers were greatly multiplied (see Acts 9:1-31).

There is a city named Kiambu in Kenya, which was described in a *Transformations* video produced by George Otis, Jr. of The Sentinel Group.[3] In this city all kinds of sin, immorality, crime, and witchcraft were going on, and no church could be successfully planted there. When a man of God went to that city, God showed him to pray until he found the gate that was causing all this. He was led to a particular shop in the High Street where a well-known witch ran a handicrafts and palmistry business. He was led to target that store and pray that the witch, along with her controlling demonic spirit, would leave town. Although she and her family had lived there for several generations, he prayed passionately for some time. Suddenly one day, she packed all her things and was gone.

The atmosphere of the entire city changed. This Christian man then started a church and began to evangelize. He soon had a church of about 2,000 people. Crime plummeted, sin and immorality almost disappeared from the city, and everything changed.

We need to target with our prayers those people who presently serve as "gates of satan." We must get to know them by name and find out where they meet, where they go, and what they do. I am talking about ardent anti-Christian secularists, sexually-perverse activists, militant atheists, witches and warlocks, the passionate promoters of New Age, the devotees of Mother Earth, and other such things. We must pray for them with love, not hate; but we must be firm, so that they might have their eyes opened. Then they can repent and be converted, and the demons will leave them. Otherwise, if they stubbornly persist in their cooperation with these spirits and their resistance to God, then it may become necessary to pray that God will take them out one way or the other. But this kind of warfare must only be done as a result of an express, specific Word from God.

This type of "gate" also includes strong activists who are demonically empowered to passionately promote political causes like abortion, homosexuality, lesbian and gay rights, the ACLU, and militant atheism. They may also promote false religions such as Wicca and secret societies like Freemasonry, Mormonism, various false cults, subtle religious deceptions, demon-based martial arts, and other such things. They are sometimes violent fanatics of another religion.

We may hate what they do, but we must not hate them as individuals. The Bible teaches that we do not wrestle against flesh and blood, but against principalities and powers and the spiritual wickedness in heavenly places that control them (see Eph. 6:12). We need to pray for their deliverance from these demonic influences and for their conversion to Jesus so that God can turn them around, just as He did the apostle Paul. When these gates are possessed by Jesus and they become ardent promoters of the Kingdom of God, a tremendous shift occurs in the spirit realm.

We must use our heavenly authority to ensure that these demons are dethroned. Either the demons leave the person and the person gets saved; or if the person won't let them go, then the person and the demons in them must leave together. Either way, they have to go! When this actually takes place, the demonic canopy of darkness over a city or an even wider region is removed and replaced by the canopy of the Kingdom of Heaven. Then everything changes for the better, and a great harvest can be reaped.

By the power of the blood Jesus shed on Calvary and by His resurrection, we have the authority and power to take back what satan has stolen from the Body of Christ. We are living in a critical time in history for the Church. It is time to take control of the gates of our minds and how we think. We must cleanse geographical regions that have been used for demonic worship and overthrow the spiritual powers that have hindered the growth and fullness of the Kingdom of God on earth. It is an exciting time to be alive, and we certainly have much work to do!

ENDNOTES

1. Albert Outler, *John Wesley's Sermons: An Anthology* (Abingdon Press, October 1991), 355. See also: http://wesley.nnu.edu/john-wesley/the-sermons-of-john-wesley-1872-edition/the-sermons-of-john-wesley-thomas-jacksons-numbering

2. Ramsay MacMullen, *Christianizing the Roman Empire (A.D. 100-400)* (New Haven, CT: Yale University Press, 1984), 26.

3. George Otis Jr, *Transformations,* video (Sentinel Group, 1999).

CHAPTER 11

FEEDING THE 5,000—A
PROPHETIC SIGN

IN order to advance God's Kingdom on Earth, we must recognize prophetic signs in our day and learn how to gain revelation from them. The best way to learn how to do this is to look at some of the prophetic signs Jesus used to teach His disciples. One such example is the miraculous feeding of the 5,000 men (besides women and children) that is recorded in all four Gospels. Shortly after this event, a similar miracle occurred when Jesus fed 4,000 men, plus women and children. (The latter is recorded only in the Gospels of Matthew and Mark.)

To fully understand these miracles, we need to study the details as presented in the various Gospels and then seek God for His revelation.

In Mark's Gospel, Jesus referred to both of these miracles while traveling in a boat with His disciples on the Sea of Galilee. He particularly mentioned the number of people who were fed and the number of loaves and fishes that were used in each case. He also made note of the vast amount of food and the number of large baskets full of uneaten fragments left over afterward.

In Mark 8:11-21 we read:

Then the Pharisees came out and began to dispute with Him, seeking from Him a sign from heaven, testing Him. But He sighed deeply in His spirit, and said, "Why does this generation seek a sign? Assuredly, I say to you, no sign shall be given to this generation." And He left them, and getting into the boat again, departed to the other side. Now the disciples had forgotten to take bread, and they did not have more than one loaf with them in the boat. Then He charged them, saying, "Take heed, beware of the leaven of the Pharisees and the leaven of Herod." And they reasoned among themselves, saying, "It is because we have no bread." But Jesus, being aware of it, said to them, "Why do you reason because you have no bread? Do you not yet perceive nor understand? Is your heart still hardened? Having eyes, do you not see? And having ears, do you not hear? And do you not remember? When I broke the five loaves for the five thousand, how many baskets full of fragments did you take up?" They said to Him, "Twelve." "Also, when I broke the seven for the four thousand, how many large baskets full of fragments did you take up?" And they said, "Seven." So He said to them, "How is it you do not understand?"

Jesus marveled at the spiritual blindness of His disciples because they did not understand the deeper significance of these miracles and of the various numbers involved. Years ago, convicted by this, I had to get on my knees before Jesus and confess that I was just as blind as they were, and I asked Him to show me what all of this meant. This led me to fast and pray, during which time He opened up to me their deeper meanings.

AVOIDING BAD LEAVEN

In the Mark 8:11-21 passage, Jesus used the analogy of making bread, an example with which everybody would be familiar. He spoke of two bad forms of leaven, or yeast, that can contaminate the whole "dough" of the Kingdom. If received, they poison the minds of people who mix them into the true bread of eating Him and really knowing Him with deep intimacy. As a result, they cannot see or understand the Kingdom properly. Altogether, in this and other places, Jesus refers to four bad kinds of leaven and one good kind, discussed below:

1) The Leaven of the Scribes and Pharisees Was Religious Legalism

They turned their religious lives into a practice of meticulously observing a multitude of rules and regulations concerning clothing, eating habits, and many outward things that they could or could not do. They were only concerned with the outward life and how they appeared before people and were not at all concerned with the condition of a person's heart.

2) The Leaven of Herod and the Herodians Was Political Correctness and Diplomatic Expediency

This was expressed in the lives of the Roman and Jewish politicians and Jewish religious leaders. They were full of diplomatic expediency and political correctness. They were also greedy for money and practiced manipulation to gain increased political power and influence.

Herod, who would do or say anything that would further his political career, was the epitome of this. He had worked hard for many years to complete the new temple in Jerusalem. However, his motive for building it was not to glorify God; he did it to gain favor with the Jewish rulers. At the same time, he had built several temples around the Roman Empire that were dedicated to the worship of Augustus Caesar. These were built to gain him favor with the Roman emperor. He was first and foremost a political animal with no true knowledge of God and no unwavering standards of truth, morality, integrity, or righteousness.

No one can truly serve God and be politically correct at the same time. When there is a conflict between the clear commandments of God and secular laws that have been passed, then we must always obey God, who is the higher authority, even if that means breaking a secular law that is contrary to His Word (see Acts 4:17-20).

3) The Leaven of the Sadducees Was Humanistic Rationalism

In Matthew's Gospel, Jesus warned of the leaven of the Sadducees as well as that of the Pharisees (see Matt. 16:6-12). The Sadducees were famous for their intellectualism, rationalism, and liberalism; they were unable to believe anything they could not understand with the rational mind. Jesus spoke of this several times. The Sadducees had great difficulties with Jesus and His teaching; they had even more problems dealing with the flow of miracles that He did.

The Sadducees rejected all the stories of miracles and anything supernatural recorded in the Old Testament Scriptures because they could not understand them intellectually. They especially did not believe in the possibility of anyone being raised from the dead, and they regarded even these Old Testament biblical stories as myths invented by people. They did not regard the Scriptures as the infallible Word of God, like the Pharisees and scribes did. As a result, they were greatly offended by Peter and later by Paul preaching Jesus and His resurrection from the dead. But even more, they were offended by the apostles' growing popularity amongst the people. So they attacked them and caused them to be arrested and thrown into jail (see Acts 4:1-3, 23:6-10).

4) The Leaven of Sin

Elsewhere, in a number of Scriptures in both the Old and New Testaments, another type of bad leaven is described: the practices of the sinful nature within our human flesh. For these reasons, at the beginning of the Feast of Passover, all leaven had to be removed from every house. All Jews had to eat unleavened bread during the eight-day Feast of Passover, which began with the sacrifice and eating of the Passover Lamb. This signified the putting away of all sin through the power of the slain Lamb of God. All of this pointed prophetically to the cross and even more to the glorious power of the resurrection life of Jesus that enables us to live free from the power of sin.

5) One Good Leaven: The Holy Spirit Leavening God's Kingdom

In Matthew 13:33, in the midst of Jesus' teaching of many parables of the Kingdom, He mentioned one good leaven, which He said was an essential part of the Kingdom. This leaven had to be added in such a way that it leavened the whole lump of "dough." This leaven allegorically represented the Holy Spirit.

The Holy Spirit must truly come into every part of our being and leaven us throughout, infusing all our being—including the way we think—with His presence and the power of Jesus' resurrection. Then the things we do can truly be part of the Kingdom.

It is interesting to note that at the Jewish Feast of Pentecost, unlike the Feast of Passover, the rules regarding eating leaven were totally different. The Feast of Pentecost coincided exactly with the barley harvest, and at this festival, all faithful Jews were *commanded to eat leavened bread,* not unleavened bread. This bread would probably have been barley bread; it is a powerful picture of our need of the Holy Spirit in all His fullness, especially as we come into the Kingdom. (See Leviticus 23:15-18.)

"When the Day of Pentecost had fully come..." (Acts 2:1), it came as usual, at the time of the barley harvest. It was on that very same day that the Holy Spirit first fell upon the Church in the upper room. As a result of that mighty anointing, the disciples burst out of that room full of the Holy Spirit and were able to powerfully preach and demonstrate that the Kingdom of God with all its power had indeed come.

THE ALLEGORY OF THE BLIND MAN

Now let us return to Mark 8:22-26. After Mark had recorded all the questions Jesus asked concerning the numbers of loaves involved in the two miracles of feeding the multitude and the number of baskets left over in each case, Mark immediately continued with the story of the blind man who was brought to

Jesus at that moment. This is the only example in Scripture where Jesus healed someone gradually, in two stages.

I want you to see that this man was an allegorical picture of the spiritual blindness of the apostles at that time. They did not understand the true significance or the allegorical meaning of these two great and very similar miracles.

They could not see the significance of the loaves, the fish, and the fragments left over or the numbers that Jesus deliberately mentioned. This blind man was brought to Jesus from Bethsaida, which means *"house of fish"*; they pleaded with Jesus to touch him. Jesus deliberately did to the blind man physically what He was about to do to the apostles spiritually. Like him, they would progressively receive their sight. There were five phases to this healing:

1. *He took him out of the village.* Just like this man, the apostles and probably all of Jesus' disciples had to be released from a "village" way of seeing things. This is true of most Christian leaders and believers today. They can only "see" and be concerned about their own needs, their own local church, and their own immediate situation. As a result, they do not really see the Kingdom in terms of cities and nations that have to be reached.

2. *At first the man only saw vague shadowy shapes.* He saw *"men like trees, walking"* (Mark 8:24). Something definitely happened when Jesus had spit in his eyes and laid hands on him. He was no longer totally blind, but the healing wasn't complete. Instead of total darkness there was now some light, but things were not really clear.

3. *The man was honest about how much he could see.* After spitting in his eyes (a picture of the power of God's creative Word) and laying His hands on the man (a picture of the power of impartation), Jesus asked him if he saw anything. He told Jesus exactly what he could now see—vague, shadowy images like

"men as trees walking." I believe that if the man had exaggerated and pretended he could see more clearly than he actually did and had said, "Oh yes, now I can really see," the healing process would have stopped there. He would have gone away still severely handicapped with only partial vision.

It is easy for Christians, when the Kingdom is being preached, to learn some of the language and learn to sing some of the songs of the Kingdom without really seeing the Kingdom clearly. If we live lives of "Kingdom talk" and pretense, if we claim to see more clearly than we actually do, we will never come to a full revelation and understanding of the glorious Kingdom of God.

4. *Jesus touched him again.* The man looked up and focused his attention as Jesus touched him again. Now he saw everything clearly. The man really wanted perfect vision, and he persisted until he got it. We must behave the same way and have the same attitude as we *"seek first the Kingdom of God and His righteousness...",* then everything else will be ours as well (Matt. 6:33).

5. *Jesus warned him not to go back to the village again.* If he did, he probably would have lost his sight again. Back in the environment of the village, he would soon be persuaded to return to his old ways of thinking and seeing in the smallness of village life.

If God opens your eyes when you are attending a great conference or reading an enlightening book or having some great experience and you come to see the Kingdom much more clearly, take care not to return to your local church or "village" way of seeing and thinking, thereby losing the vision that God has supernaturally given you. Mentally, you must come out of the village and stay out of it!

GETTING READY FOR THE MULTITUDE

According to Matthew 9:35-38, Jesus was overwhelmed with a great multitude and their tremendous needs. He earnestly said, *"The harvest truly is plentiful, but the laborers are few"* (Matt. 9:37). Immediately afterward, because of His great compassion for the people, He appointed the 12 apostles and sent them out (see Matt. 10:1).

Many flocked to Him in those days to get their needs met, but only a few became His disciples. The largest number of actual disciples of Jesus that was ever mentioned in Scripture was the 500 who saw Him at one time after His resurrection. There were only 120 disciples who literally obeyed Jesus' command and were still waiting in the upper room on the Day of Pentecost when the Spirit fell. Where were the rest of them?

When Jesus was preaching and healing the multitude, there were tens of thousands present; but in His more private, intimate times of teaching His disciples the numbers were always quite small, most often it was only the 12.

FEEDING THE 5,000—ITS DEEPER MEANING AND PURPOSE

In the sixth chapter of John's Gospel, the rich allegorical purpose of the miracle of feeding the 5,000 is explained by Jesus at a much deeper level.

A multitude had gathered to hear Jesus teach and to be healed. They had been with Him for some time and were becoming hungry. We are told in the various Gospels there were 5,000 men besides women and children. That would probably mean a crowd of at least 20,000 people.

They urgently needed feeding, so in John 6:5 Jesus asked Philip a test question about feeding the crowd. Jesus wanted to see what His disciple would do. Philip could only respond naturally and realized he was facing an impossible situation. How could even a little food be obtained for so many? Even 100 denarii, which was 100 days' wages for a skilled workman and probably equivalent to about $15,000 today, wouldn't go very far among 20,000 hungry people. But Jesus already knew what He would do.

This miracle took place just before the Feast of Passover, one year before Jesus was crucified. It was performed by Jesus so as to be a powerful example of the kind of Church that these apostles would soon be leading. Its purpose was to show them how they would have to be organized in order to feed the great harvest that would soon be reaped once the Day of Pentecost had come.

Jesus first determined what resources they had. There was one lad with five small barley loaves and two fishes. This lad himself was an allegorical picture of the individual apostles who spiritually were still like immature children in the eyes of Jesus. This was a term which Jesus affectionately used several times when addressing the apostles. He literally called them "lads." It was used partly to show His affection and partly to underline their immaturity and lack of spiritual understanding until the Spirit came. (For example, see John 21:5, when Jesus appeared to the apostles for the third time after His resurrection. He literally asked, *"Children, have you any food?"*)

The five loaves and two fishes were intended for one little boy's lunch, and the loaves would have been very small, like biscuits. I believe that these five barley loaves represent the Ephesians 4:11 fivefold ministries; the fishes, which gave flavor and protein content to the food, allegorically represented the new converts whose joy and freshness would add a delightful meaty, spicy flavor to church life. Without a steady flow of such new converts, church life can quickly become very stale and dull.

Barley was normally grown to feed cattle. Only poor people would buy barley and make it into bread for human consumption. This speaks of our need to be "poor" in spirit in order to see the Kingdom. Jesus said, *"Blessed are the poor in spirit, for theirs is the kingdom of heaven"* (Matt. 5:3).

As we have already seen, barley was closely connected to the Feast of Pentecost. It was the first of the several grain harvests which were reaped consecutively during the summer months. Barley was reaped at exactly the same time as the Feast of Pentecost. For these reasons, barley is often an allegory, or type of the Holy Spirit, and there are many delightful examples of this in the Scriptures, which we cannot fully cover here.

Jesus then told the apostles to instruct the multitude to sit down on the rich grass in companies of 50 to 100 men, with their families. There must have been about 80 such companies, with 100 to 400 in each, including women and children, making up one large multitude of about 20,000.

The apostles came to Jesus, and He broke each of the five loaves into small pieces, along with tiny fragments from the two fish, and put a small piece of bread and fish into each of their hands. He then told them to go to each company and begin to distribute the food.

Jesus deliberately made the obedience of the apostles part of the miracle and so forced them to act in faith. As they went from Jesus to their first company, all that they had in their hands was one small fragment of bread and one tiny fragment of fish. It must have seemed totally inadequate to feed even one person, let alone this vast multitude.

It wasn't until they began to give out these little scraps in dogged faith that the miracle of multiplication began to happen before their eyes, probably to their utter amazement. They kept on giving out the fragments, which were multiplying as they gave them out. Everybody kept eating, and the fragments kept on multiplying until all the people were full. When the remaining uneaten fragments were gathered up, there were many times more left over than they had started with.

What the disciples didn't know then was that in just over a year from the day that Jesus performed this miracle, they would begin spiritually feeding the first city church in Jerusalem. Incredibly, the numbers would rapidly increase to about the same number of 20,000 people within approximately two years.

It would be one city church of many congregations with the apostles moving among these many companies of believers, who would meet in many different places and in various ways. The apostles would train and release Ephesians 4:11 ministries as fast as they could in order to feed all these hungry people spiritually. On that day, they would be doing spiritually what they had done physically the year before—and it would be equally miraculous. The vision Zechariah saw would be literally fulfilled in Jerusalem! The miracle which Jesus performed was a prophetic parable of what was about to happen to the Church in Jerusalem.

THE SIGNIFICANCE OF THE NUMBERS

One more thing we must note is that everything about this miracle was in *fives* and *twelves*. Numerology is a topic which needs to be kept in balance. It can be taken to such extremes that it can become very unbalanced and even erroneous. However, we must recognize the fact that certain numbers in Scripture have special significance and some definite allegorical or prophetic meanings.

Everything to do with the Jewish Scriptures, which we now call the Old Testament, is in *fives* and *twelves*. We have five books of the Law, twelve books of History, five books of Poetry, five Major Prophets, and twelve Minor Prophets, making up thirty-nine Books of the Old Testament. There are other examples of this.

It seems to me that it was very fitting that the first city church, a Jewish church in Jerusalem, should be portrayed in terms of *fives* and *twelves*. Its primary sphere of ministry was to first reach Jerusalem and then reach out to Jewish communities everywhere in the world and proclaim to them the coming of their long-expected Messiah and His glorious Kingdom.

Much was accomplished by Barnabas and Peter as they went to Jewish communities all over the Roman Empire. In addition, we know from other, non-biblical records that Matthew went to the Jewish communities in Ethiopia and other parts of North Africa, and Thomas went to similar Jewish trading communities in Southern India—in Kerala and in Tamil Nadu around the city now called Chennai. This all took place within a couple of decades of the Church being born on the Day of Pentecost. They made many converts from the Jewish residents and also some local native proselytes as they established churches there.

In the feeding of the 4,000 men, four loaves were used to feed 4,000 men, besides women and children, comprising another multitude of about 16,000 people. Seven large baskets full of fragments were left over. Everything in this miracle was *fours* and *sevens*. What does this mean?

I want to suggest to you that four is widely accepted as the universal number symbolizing the four corners of the earth. Seven is the number of perfection. By this second miracle, I believe that Jesus was prophesying the formation of a second mighty city church and apostolic center at Antioch, which would be raised up among the Gentiles, to send the Gospel to the four corners of the earth. To Jesus this would be the perfect, complete fulfillment of His heart; it was what Jesus had commanded His disciples when He told them to go into all the world and make disciples of all nations.

THE GOSPEL IS FOR ALL NATIONS

Within a few years, the Gospel of the Kingdom ran over the wall from Judea, first into Samaria, and from there into the Gentile world beginning at Antioch. This was where Barnabas brought the newly-established apostle Paul to teach for a whole year. This was also where believers were first called *Christianoi,* meaning "little Christs." The name developed because they so clearly replicated the life of Jesus—and everybody in the city could see it. (See Acts 11:19-26.)

Here in Antioch, a second great city church was established with a powerful multiracial group of apostles, prophets, and teachers. These leaders were made up of Jews, proselytes, and Gentiles, some of whom were black North Africans, Arabians, and Europeans. One was called Simeon the Niger (literally "the black") and another was named Lucius. Both men came from Cyrene, a city that was located in present-day Libya, in North Africa.

From Antioch, apostolic teams went out under Paul's leadership to Philippi, Thessalonica, Berea, Athens, Corinth, and many other places. In several of these cities, additional city churches were established that in turn became powerful apostolic centers reaching out to their whole region and planting many new churches.

Ephesus, a major city in the Roman Empire, was the home of the great temple to Diana, the pagan goddess mentioned earlier who dominated the spiritual darkness of the Roman Empire. As we have seen, this spirit had been in Paul's spiritual gunsights for some time, but he had to go through a special process of preparation and training before he was ready for that level of conflict. Paul was the apostle the Lord chose to go take the Gospel to the Gentiles; Ephesus was one of the foremost of the Asian churches apostolically led by Paul.

I hope you have gleaned fresh revelation from our study of the miracles Jesus performed. In these days, we must have eyes to see beyond the physical and into the spiritual realm to discern what the Spirit is saying. The best way to learn how to do this is to look at what Jesus did in His day. We will continue this study of His miracles in the next chapter.

ENDNOTE

1. *Blue Letter Bible,* "Dictionary and Word Search for *Bethsaïda* (Strong's 966)," 1996-2011, http://www.blueletterbible.org/lang/lexicon/lexicon.cfm?Strongs=G966&t=KJV; accessed June 13, 2011.

CHAPTER 12

SEEKING THE TRUE BREAD FROM HEAVEN

IT is amazing how many key principles can be discovered when studying just one of the miracles Jesus performed, such as the feeding of 5,000 people. Let us go back to John 6:15-68 and look at another great truth.

After Jesus had fed the multitude, He sent them away. He then went up into the mountains to pray, having already sent the disciples over to the other side of the Lake of Galilee in a boat. The disciples ran into a violent storm in the middle of the lake and were in danger of sinking, but Jesus came to them walking on the water.

When they arrived at Capernaum on the other side of the lake, the multitude He sent away near Tiberias somehow found out where He had gone and followed Him there in boats. Jesus rightly discerned that they were not seeking Him for spiritual reasons, but were eager for another free meal. He then exhorted them in John 6:27: *"Do not labor for the food which perishes, but for the food which endures to everlasting life which the Son of Man will give you...."*

They responded by asking Him what they must do to be able to work the works of God. In light of their self-focused motives for seeking Him, they may well have asked this question because they were thinking of the miracle which

Jesus had just done and how powerful and rich they would become if they could do the same thing whenever they wanted. Jesus once again sought to teach them to be hungry for spiritual truth, not just their immediate, material needs. He replied that doing the works of God came through their belief in Him as sent from the Father into the world.

They continued only to think in natural terms, immediately asking Him to perform another sign. They even quoted the Scriptures referring to the manna, which God supernaturally provided for their forefathers on a daily basis in the wilderness, implying that it was the bread from Heaven given by God to keep them alive. Jesus strongly refuted the idea that the manna their forefathers collected in the wilderness was the true bread from Heaven, although it did miraculously keep them physically alive for almost 40 years.

MANNA IS NOT THE TRUE BREAD

Jesus immediately began to teach them that He Himself was the *True Bread* which the Father had sent down from Heaven. He explained that His purpose was to give life to the world. They responded by crying out to Jesus to always give them this bread, but they didn't really understand what they were asking for.

Jesus then carefully set out to explain what this bread really is and how we can eat and drink of Him in such a way that He becomes part of us, supernaturally. We have to learn how to spiritually eat Him and drink Him continuously in such a way that every fiber of our being is now energized and empowered by His risen life. As a result, His life can flow out of us to be a source of power and blessing able to meet the needs of people all around us.

Jesus used these natural terms, such as eating His flesh and drinking His blood, to try to explain this deep spiritual mystery. However, He was careful to say that the words He was speaking were spirit and life and must not be taken naturally or literally. The Jews quarreled and asked, *"How can this Man give us His flesh to eat?"* (John 6:52). Now read Jesus' reply in John 6:53-58:

Then Jesus said to them, "Most assuredly, I say to you, unless you eat the flesh of the Son of Man and drink His blood, you have no life in you. Whoever eats My flesh and drinks My blood has eternal life, and I will raise him up at the last day. For My flesh is food indeed, and My blood is drink indeed. He who eats My flesh and drinks My blood abides in Me, and I in him. As the living Father sent Me, and I live because of the Father, so he who feeds on Me will live because of Me. This is the bread which came down from heaven—not as your fathers ate the manna, and are dead. He who eats this bread will live forever."

Unfortunately, even many of His disciples could only receive what He was saying in natural, literal terms and were offended. We read that after this *"many of His disciples went back and walked with Him no more"* (John 6:66).

IF ANYONE IS THIRSTY

In a similar way, on the last great day of the Feast of Tabernacles, Jesus cried out in great frustration. He was watching the Jewish priests leading the people through the special ceremony on the last day when they commemorated the miraculous provision of water that occurred when Moses struck the rock in the wilderness. They were also anticipating the occasion when they would sit down with Abraham as their host at the great feast that would take place at the end of the age. They could not see that Jesus allegorically was the Rock that had followed them; nor could they see that He, not Abraham, was the host of that great feast, which actually was going to be the great Marriage Feast of the Lamb, who was Jesus, and His glorious Bride, the Church.

In John 7:37-46 Jesus helped them to understand:

On the last day, that great day of the feast, Jesus stood and cried out, saying, "If anyone thirsts, let him come to Me and drink. He who believes in Me, as the Scripture has said, out of his heart will flow rivers of living water." But this He spoke concerning the Spirit, whom those believing in

Him would receive; for the Holy Spirit was not yet given, because Jesus was not yet glorified. Therefore many from the crowd, when they heard this saying, said, "Truly this is the Prophet." Others said, "This is the Christ." But some said, "Will the Christ come out of Galilee? Has not the Scripture said that the Christ comes from the seed of David and from the town of Bethlehem, where David was?" So there was a division among the people because of Him. Now some of them wanted to take Him, but no one laid hands on Him. Then the officers came to the chief priests and Pharisees, who said to them, "Why have you not brought Him?" The officers answered, "No man ever spoke like this Man!"

In John 7:37-38 every verb is in the present continuous tense, which means it is something we do and go on doing continually without ceasing. A literal paraphrase would read something like this: "If anyone is thirsty and goes on continually being thirsty, and comes to Me and goes on continually coming to Me, and drinks and goes on continually drinking; and if he also believes in Me and goes on continually believing in Me that I am really as big and as glorious as the Scriptures say I am, then out of his innermost being will flow out and go on continually flowing out, rivers of living water."

If we all literally obeyed this Scripture, there would be enough living water flowing out of each one of us to quench the thirst of the whole world. Jesus also said that this would be possible once the Spirit had been given.

Once again the heart of Jesus is that we should come to Him, not just to get our own needs met, but in order to have God's vast resources flowing continually into us so that they can then continually flow out of us as great rivers of healing, deliverance, and life—able to continually meet the needs of the people all around us.

UPPER ROOM LAST SUPPER DISCOURSE

When Jesus sat with His disciples in the upper room at the Last Supper, He once again tried to get them to understand what He had shown them in the great miracle of the feeding of the 5,000 men plus women and children. He first explained His own relationship with the Father while He was a Man on Earth. He had lived in His humanity by His continuous spiritual eating and drinking of the Father and of the Holy Spirit; they had been the source of His life and of the power that flowed out of Him. He had literally lived by them, and it was His deep communion with the Father and the Holy Spirit that had caused such mighty works and words to flow out of Him to bless multitudes of people.

He then explained that after His resurrection, the Spirit would truly show the Father to them, and they would be able to know the Father just as Jesus knew Him (see John 16:25-27). Furthermore, Jesus said that if they loved Him and obeyed Him as He had loved and obeyed the Father, then all three Persons of the Godhead would come and dwell within the disciples' humanity—just as the Father and the Spirit had dwelt within the humanity of Jesus (see John 14:16-17, 23-25). As a result, they would do the same works and even greater works than He had done during His life on Earth, by the power of that Risen Life within them (see John 14:12).

YOU CHOOSE: MANNA OR THE TRUE BREAD OF HEAVEN?

In most of present-day Western Christianity, the majority of regular church activity is aimed at seeking God to get our personal needs met.

Moses and the children of Israel wandered in the wilderness for almost 40 years. For most of that time, God provided them with a miraculous daily provision of manna, which they each gathered for themselves. He also miraculously caused their clothes and shoes to not wear out. It certainly wasn't luxurious living, but it kept them alive.

When they crossed over into the Promised Land, the manna immediately ceased. In the wilderness, each one had gathered manna for himself and sought only to meet his own needs and those of his immediate family. It was miraculous, but it was also totally self-centered.

When the tabernacle of Moses was completed, it traveled with them and continued with them for several hundred years after they came into the Promised Land. Once again, they went to the tabernacle primarily to get their basic needs met. Each person went on their own to seek God for themselves. The three main reasons they went to the tabernacle were:

1. To get their sins forgiven through animal sacrifices

2. To bring their tithes and offerings so they could be materially blessed

3. To be prayed for by the priests so they could be physically healed.

Unfortunately, this is what largely goes on in much of modern church life. Some people describe a "good church" as one that tries to meet all the perceived needs of its members and their families so they are happy with the service provided. It also enables them to come to God for the same three reasons outlined above:

1. To get their sins forgiven and their hurts and offenses healed

2. To bring their tithes and offerings so that God will bless them financially and materially

3. To be prayed for by the pastor or one of his ministry team so they can be healed and have any needs met.

This is what I have come to call "manna Christianity," and today many good Christian people see this as the "true bread" and the main reason for being a church member and regularly attending church.

John 6:30-34 records Jesus' words when He spoke categorically to His followers who were looking only for their own needs to be met when they asked Him for a sign:

They said to Him, "What sign will You perform then, that we may see it and believe You? What work will You do? Our fathers ate the manna in the desert; as it is written, 'He gave them bread from heaven to eat.'" Then Jesus said to them, "Most assuredly, I say to you, Moses did not give you the bread from heaven, but My Father gives you the true bread from heaven. For the bread of God is He who comes down from heaven and gives life to the world." Then they said to Him, "Lord, give us this bread always."

Jesus forced those first disciples to think and act differently. To ensure they could be better recipients of the true bread from Heaven, Jesus spent a lot of time teaching and showing them the truth found in these mighty allegorical miracles about the *true bread* and the *living water* so they could become great receivers.

The goal of Jesus was to make them see beyond simply receiving to get their own needs met. He wanted them to seek God so they would have an abundant supply for the needy multitudes around them. He wanted them to learn to draw from the vast, unlimited resources of God Himself. The primary purpose was to be able to pour this out to meet the needs of others. If they did this, He assured them they would still have plenty left over for their own needs as well.

In the feeding of the 5,000 men plus women and children, Jesus showed them how it could be done. He longed for them to live like Him—to seek to feed and drink hungrily and thirstily upon all the fullness of God just as He had done. Then they could be rivers of life and blessing to the world.

The first city churches functioned like this. As a result, they reaped a great harvest of God-hungry people, and they had a mighty transforming impact upon their pagan societies as Scripture and early Church history so wonderfully record. May God enable us to return to such a way of living that this once again becomes normal church life—the kind that changes our world the way they changed theirs.

In these mighty miracles of feeding the multitude, Jesus also forced the disciples to be the source of supply by the activation of their own faith. By causing the miracles of multiplication to be accomplished through their hands, He deliberately made them to be intermediaries. Nothing happened visibly until they themselves stepped out in obedience to do what Jesus had commanded them to do.

Let's cry out to God to deliver us and many of those in our churches from "manna Christianity" so we can once again eat the *true bread* that came down from Heaven and gave life to the world. May we be hungry and thirsty to eat His flesh and drink His blood spiritually so we have an abundance of His life within us to give away to many other people in need. May we not be offended by this revelation the way many were who no longer walked with Him after He revealed it. Rather, may we, like Peter, respond to His question, "Will you also go away?" with the same reply saying, "Lord, to whom shall we go? We are certain, and we are sure that you have the words of eternal life. And, we believe and know that You are the Christ, the Son of the Living God" (see John 6:67-69).

Since the Spirit has already been given and Jesus has already been glorified, may we also develop a lifestyle according to John 7:37-39 in which we continually seek the *true bread* from Heaven and drink of Him.

CHAPTER 13

CONFRONTING MAJOR
DEMONIC PRINCIPALITIES

SPIRITUAL warfare is a serious matter. Before we start confronting demonic forces or principalities on any level, we need to learn a few new truths. The life of Jesus is our pattern, and the Scriptures provide principles that will both protect us and show us how to win the battles the Lord tells us to fight.

First of all, we need to learn that there are multitudes of rank-and-file demonic spirits that love to torment people and inflict sicknesses upon them. More importantly, we need to understand that these demons can be removed by true believers who know how to use their authority in Jesus. In addition to this, there are also major demonic principalities to whom satan has given rule over whole regions of the earth. These demons hate Jesus and resist the coming of His Kingdom with all their might. They are passionately committed to maintaining their rule of darkness as long as they can.

To cast down these major ruling spirits requires a different order of power and authority. Jesus several times likened this power and authority to moving a demonic "mountain" by speaking to it with faith-filled authority. In Mark 9:14-29 we read of one such occasion when Jesus was speaking to His defeated disciples. They had recently seen great success in casting out ordinary rank-and-file demons when He had sent them out to heal the sick, cast out demons, and proclaim that the Kingdom had come. But after their return, they had failed to cast out a higher-ranking demon that had rule over a demonized boy. Jesus told them that they were unable to succeed because of their unbelief; He then explained, *"This kind can come out by nothing but prayer and fasting"* (Mark 9:29). Because Jesus was already living such a life, He was able to simply speak a word to this demon and immediately it had to leave.

A wonderful Disney cartoon movie made some years ago was surprisingly accurate in its biblical content. It was called *The Prince of Egypt* and told the biblical stories of Moses. The final spiritual battle between Moses and the magicians of Egypt was powerfully and vividly portrayed. This battle is recorded in Exodus 8:16-19. In the final stage of this battle, Moses came into direct conflict with the principle ruling demonic spirit which was working powerfully through these magicians. At this point in the Disney movie, the magicians confidently sing out, "You're playing with the Big Boys now." These magicians were totally confident that, by the power of the demonic spirit which they served, they would be able to outmatch and outpower anything that Moses could do.

To their surprise and horror, they suddenly found themselves rendered completely powerless and unable to do anything before the supernatural power of the Holy Spirit working through Moses. The Bible records the magicians' cries at that point: "This is none other than the finger of God" (see Exod. 8:19). They became helpless and powerless spectators of the power flowing through Moses. They were unable to do anything except watch Moses continue to do great miracles before Pharaoh by the superior power of Moses' God, Jehovah.

In Luke 11:20-22, Jesus said:

> But if I cast out demons with the finger of God, surely the kingdom of God has come upon you. When a strong man, fully armed, guards his own palace, his goods are in peace. But when a stronger than he comes upon him and overcomes him, he takes from him all his armor in which he trusted, and divides his spoils.

By this statement, Jesus clearly declared that someone moving in the power of the Kingdom of God is stronger than any demonic "strong man" that had previously felt secure and at peace in what he had regarded as his own territory. He then declared that those with real Kingdom authority had power to "rob him of all his goods." To be successful at this level of spiritual warfare, we have to learn the five lessons that Paul learned on his journey through Macedonia and Achaia.

Initially, Paul tried to go into Asia straight from his successful tour through Cyprus and Pisidia after being sent out from Antioch. He had rightly discerned that a major demonic principality was resident in Ephesus. It was seriously hindering the forceful advance of the Kingdom over the whole of the Roman Empire and needed to be cast down. This was the mighty demonic force that emanated from the great temple of Diana in Ephesus.

In the days of Augustus Caesar, this temple had been greatly enlarged and had become one of the Seven Wonders of the World. This spirit was worshiped throughout the Roman Empire; political leaders, military generals, and prominent businessmen came to Ephesus from great distances to worship this "god," seeking its favor and blessing upon their lives and activities. The temple had formerly been dedicated to Artemis in the days of the Greek Empire. It was then dedicated to Diana during the period of the Roman Empire, which was another name for the same spirit.

This same demonic principality had formerly ruled over several of the preceding great civilizations and empires under various names as far back as Baal of the Babylonian and the Persian-Median Empires. During the days of the Egyptian Empire, this demonic principality was known as the great "goddess" Isis.

It is very probable that as Paul planned to go into Asia and to Ephesus, its major city, he was about to confront the same spirit which had worked through the magicians of Egypt and opposed Moses in the days of Pharaoh.

When Paul initially tried to go straight to Ephesus, we read in Acts 16 that he was *"forbidden by the Holy Spirit to preach the word in Asia"* (Acts 16:6). He then tried to go into Bithynia, which was the northern part of the same area, and again *"the Spirit did not permit them"* (Acts 16:7). Finally, in the night, he received a vision of a man from Macedonia who called out for Paul to come and help them (see Acts 16:9-10). We read that, in this case and others, Paul was not disobedient to the heavenly vision (see Acts 26:19) and went to Macedonia and Achaia where he learned some valuable lessons which prepared him to make a successful assault on Ephesus several years later.

These lessons can be summarized as follows:

1) THE LESSON OF PHILIPPI (ACTS 16:11-40)

Paul first came to Philippi, the foremost city of that part of Macedonia, and found a place by the river where prayer was customarily made by a group of women on the Sabbath. They were probably Jews, or at least Jewish proselytes. As he talked to them, Lydia, who was a seller of purple cloth, responded immediately. She and her household were baptized.

There was then a violent backlash from the owners of a slave girl from whom Paul cast out a spirit of divination. Paul and Silas were badly beaten and cast into prison. Instead of falling into depression and despair as John the Baptist had done in similar circumstances, they defiantly worshiped and praised God in spite of their circumstances. As a result, they saw a powerful, supernatural transformation of the whole situation. The prison was shaken with a powerful earthquake, everybody was set free, and the jailer and his family were converted. Paul and Silas literally praised their way out of prison. However, Paul could not stay in that city and had to move on to another place.

The lesson they learned in Philippi was not to give up in adverse circumstances or go into depression and defeat because of a painful setback where the devil seemed to be winning. Instead, by dogged faith, they were to worship and praise God as Lord and were to continue to see Him on His throne having all power and authority, in spite of the circumstances.

2) THE LESSON OF THESSALONICA (ACTS 17:1-9)

Paul then left Philippi in a measure of triumph and went to Thessalonica. Once again he saw a powerful breakthrough, particularly among the devout Greeks and leading women, with many being healed and delivered from demons. Paul testified how these new converts marvelously turned from idols to serve the living God and became zealous imitators of Paul as he imitated Christ (see 1 Thess. 1:9, 6). In three powerful weeks, the city was shaken and so changed that they soon began to send out missionaries of their own all over Macedonia and Achaia.

As a result Paul was able to testify to them later that their faith had gone out to the whole region so that he didn't need to say anything (see 1 Thess. 1:6-9). However, after those blessed three weeks, violent opposition arose from the Jews, and Paul and Silas had to be sent away by night to Berea.

The lesson he learned in Thessalonica was that people who have been worshiping idols are bound to be demon-possessed. Paul and his team learned to cast out those demons immediately and completely. They could not allow these new converts to come into the Church in that condition and cause so many problems.

We learned the very same things in India. You can be sure that those who have been worshiping idols or seeking the power of the occult, including casting spells and obtaining healings, will be demon-possessed and in need of deliverance.

In these days, in America and in many European nations, we find many people have had contact with the demonic through their drug use, engaging in sexual promiscuity, experimenting with the occult, dabbling in witchcraft, exploring other mystic religions, practicing yoga or martial arts, or being actively involved in Freemasonry. As a result, they need to be delivered from demons as soon as they come to Christ. In these days, deliverance must be established in our churches to ensure new converts are completely delivered from their earliest days as Christians, just as Paul did in Thessalonica.

3) THE LESSON OF BEREA (ACTS 17:10-14)

When Paul came to Berea, he experienced a much more reasonable and open reception. We read in Acts 17:11 that the Jews in Berea were more fair-minded than the violent Jews in Thessalonica, and they gave Paul a fair hearing. But before they responded to him, they first searched the Scriptures for themselves to see if the things he taught were really so. *Paul learned here that all his new revelation concerning Jesus and the Kingdom had to be solidly based upon Scripture and provable from Scripture* if he was going to avoid persecution from the Jews.

I learned the same thing as a fairly new missionary in India in the early 1960s. It was after my baptism in the Holy Spirit, when I began to see all these glorious new things that God was showing me concerning the Kingdom of God. I was working with some wonderful, seasoned Brethren missionaries who were full of the knowledge of the Word, but were without the Spirit's power. I soon discovered that everything I said was tested by these faithful Bible-based missionaries to see if it was truly scriptural. It forced me to carefully search the Scriptures myself and make sure I was solidly Bible-based in all I taught and practiced.

This same training has continued to keep me thoroughly Bible-based today and has prevented me from veering off into error. Over my many years in ministry, I have tragically seen a number of individuals, and some promising movements, go wrong and into error because this important principle was not carefully observed.

Instead, some people began majoring on a particular ecstatic experience rather than the solid truth of Scripture. Some of these "experiences" later turned out to be subtle deceptions of the devil. They caused a lot of problems and brought discredit to the real things that God was doing.

Notwithstanding his open reception in Berea, after a short time, Paul was again driven out of town when some violent Jews from Thessalonica came to Berea and stirred up severe opposition against him. Again Paul had to leave hurriedly. He went to Athens, leaving Silas and Timothy behind in Berea.

4) THE LESSON OF ATHENS (ACTS 17:15-34)

While Paul was waiting in Athens for Silas and Timothy, he had time to observe the tremendous religious life and vast number of temples that offered almost infinite paths to "god." There was even a temple to "the unknown god."

Athens throbbed with a strong demonic mixture of intellectualism and syncretism. Their Greek-based, human philosophy had a façade of intellectual brilliance and tolerance, but was full of subtle demonic deception.

Paul was deeply stirred in his spirit and felt he must do something about this terrible spiritual blindness and darkness. He stood on Mars Hill at the center of all this and began to preach. His message, recorded in full for us in Acts 17:22-31, was a masterpiece of skillful and culturally-relevant oratory. He was even able to relate to the people's ethnicity and culture and quoted their poets so as to be more acceptable.

Things seemed to be going well until he mentioned the resurrection of Jesus from the dead. At that point, the crowd laughed him to scorn and refused to listen anymore. Very few believed, and the vast majority moved away to hear a more interesting speaker. Athens was the only place on this whole tour where there was such a response. Unlike other places, there was no revival and very few were saved; neither was there a riot. No significant church was established and almost nothing happened.

Soon afterward, Paul left Athens and began to walk the long road to Corinth, a journey of about 70 miles. I can imagine him on the way asking God, "What went wrong? Why did so little happen in Athens? Why was there no powerful breakthrough?"

The response of the Holy Spirit must have been something like this: "Paul, you didn't preach the cross."

If you review that great piece of oratory which Paul preached on Mars Hill, there is no mention of the cross anywhere. Perhaps he thought such preaching was too foolish for those intellectuals and decided to try a more rational approach. This was his big mistake, and he clearly learned his lesson by the time he reached Corinth.

After arriving in Corinth, Paul told the people:

> *And I, brethren, when I came to you, did not come with excellence of speech or of wisdom declaring to you the testimony of God. For I determined not to know anything among you except Jesus Christ and Him crucified. I was with you in weakness, in fear, and in much trembling. And my speech and my preaching were not with the persuasive words of human wisdom, but in demonstration of the Spirit and of power, that your faith should not be in the wisdom of men but in the power of God* (1 Corinthians 2:1-5).

5) THE LESSONS OF CORINTH (ACTS 18:1-18)

We have already seen that Paul thoroughly learned his lesson from his mistakes in Athens and had already determined how he would preach the Gospel in Corinth. He didn't make the same mistake again. He only preached the "foolishness" of the cross in the power of the Spirit (see 1 Cor. 1:17-18).

Corinth was the second largest city of the Roman Empire. It was the chief city of Achaia, the major port, the commercial center, and, apart from Rome itself, the most cosmopolitan city of the Roman Empire.

As we have seen, during his journey throughout the region of Macedonia and Achaia (with the exception of the city of Athens), Paul's ministry led to an initial spiritual breakthrough followed by attacks and riots caused by hostile Jews. In each case, he was then brought before the Roman authorities at the judgment seat and every judgment went against him. He was either beaten and thrown into jail or beaten and thrown out of the city before any church had been properly established.

We need to remember that Paul never enjoyed the privileges of the first 12 apostles; having walked with Jesus for over three years, they saw and heard first-hand everything He did or said. These apostles were also with Jesus at the Last Supper and heard His last great discourse the night before He was arrested and crucified. This was recorded for us many years later in John 13–17.

Unlike them, Paul did not see Jesus after He was risen from the dead, did not hear Him teach on the Kingdom of God for the 40 days after His resurrection and before He ascended to His Father. Nor was he with the original apostles in the upper room for those ten days before the Spirit fell upon each one of them on the Day of Pentecost.

Particularly, in this context, Paul did not hear the last commandment that Jesus gave His disciples just before He ascended to His Father, when He told them they should wait or, more accurately, sit down, in Jerusalem until they were clothed with power from on high. The Greek word *kathidzo* is translated "tarry" in the New King James Version of Luke 24:49; it literally means to "sit down."[1] The great truth of this verse is better paraphrased as follows: "You apostles must learn to sit down with Me, in all My risen authority, upon My throne and you must stay in Jerusalem until you are clothed with power from on high."

Obviously, Paul would have learned many things from his dialogue with the other apostles when he spent time with them in Jerusalem. But he still lacked knowledge and understanding in some areas; this was one of them. So several times Jesus came to him in a vision and personally rectified this lack of knowledge by teaching Paul Himself.

Paul records three occasions when Jesus appeared to him and instructed him personally as to what he should preach so as to make up for that lack of not being present with the other apostles. It is interesting to note the three things Jesus focused on during those personal appearances to Paul.

The first was concerning the content of his Gospel message to the Galatians. Paul mentioned the revelation in his letter to the Galatians and declared that he received it directly from Jesus and not from any man (see Gal. 1:9-12). He summarized the content of his God-given Gospel message again in his testimony before Felix in Acts 26:14-19. Please especially note verse 18:

> To open their eyes, in order to turn them from darkness to light, and from the power of Satan to God, that they may receive forgiveness of sins and an inheritance among those who are sanctified by faith in Me.

It covers five major principles and three things which have to precede the joy of offering a lost sinner forgiveness of sins. When I came to understand this myself, it changed significantly the way that I preached the Gospel; and it produced a much higher percentage of life-transforming conversions.

The second revelation Paul mentioned as having been personally shown to him by Jesus was one which Paul taught to the Corinthians regarding how they should participate in the communion. He taught them what Jesus had showed him, explaining what the ordinance really signified, and the great power it contained when received properly by faith (see 1 Cor. 11:23-30).

On the third occasion, Jesus appeared to Paul in Corinth after he had begun to preach there. Paul had joined forces with Aquila and Priscilla because they were of the same tent-making trade as Paul. When Timothy and Silas had also joined him there, he felt a strong compulsion to preach and began to do so, first in the synagogue to both Jews and Greeks, and later in the house of Justus.

Many responded and were converted and then baptized. But once again, there was a strong, violent reaction from the orthodox Jews. It looked like Paul's experience in several other cities was about to be repeated; he would be beaten by the mob, arrested by the authorities, and either thrown into jail or thrown out of the city.

However, that night Jesus appeared to Paul in a vision and said to him: "Do not be afraid, but speak, and do not keep silent; for I am with you, and no one will attack you to hurt you; for I have many people in this city" (Acts 18:9-10). Unfortunately the next verse, verse 11, is not well translated in most English versions. The word which is translated "he continued" in verse 11 in most translations is again the

Greek word *kathidzo*. A much better translation would be "he sat down there." A good paraphrase of Acts 18:11 would be: "Paul was able to continue because he chose to sit down with Jesus on His throne and exercise the authority of that throne by faith over the civil authorities of that city so they could not throw him out as had previously been done in other cities." Paul remained in the city, in spite of the opposition, for another year and six months.

Then things got even worse; the Jews rose up against Paul and dragged him to the judgment seat. However, Paul had so thoroughly learned his lesson that, in his spirit, he remained seated with authority on the throne with Jesus. The throne of Jesus was far above the judgment seat of Rome in power and authority. As it happened, Paul didn't need to speak to defend himself. Gallio, the Roman proconsul of Achaia, was moved by the power of that heavenly throne of Jesus to bring a just verdict in favor of Paul against the Jews. So Gallio dismissed the charges, and Paul was acquitted to continue many more days in Corinth (see Acts 18:12-18). As a result, a very large church was established in Corinth.

Now that *Paul had learned to use that authority and remain seated with Christ on His throne,* he was able to cause the authority of the Roman judicial courts to work in his favor. During the rest of his ministry, Paul was never again thrown out of any city by an illegal judgment of any Roman official.

Now his training was complete, and he was ready for battle with the spirit of Diana, the major demonic principality throughout the Roman Empire. God then opened the door for him to go from Corinth to Ephesus.

The lesson we must learn from all this is that warfare with major demonic principalities is very much a part of the Christian experience, but it is not for novices. Like Paul, we must be careful to hear the Holy Spirit and go through whatever training is necessary and only move into battles when we have received a definite word from God that it is time to go.

THE ASSAULT ON EPHESUS BEGINS (ACTS 18:19-19:21)

In these verses we read how the initial breakthrough in Ephesus took place. We will do well to learn these lessons carefully as we seek similar breakthroughs in our cities. We will have to deal with many similar situations before we see real transformation.

Step #1: Establish a Basic Prayer Group (Acts 19:1-7)

You've probably already noticed that in almost all of the cities that Paul visited on his tour through Macedonia and Achaia, the first contact he made was with a group of praying people. They were always the first to respond to his message, and they readily received the *good news* concerning Jesus and His Kingdom. The prayer group then became the powerhouse from which the power of God broke forth upon the city in mighty signs, wonders, and miracles.

When Paul arrived in Ephesus, it was no different. He made a quick exploratory visit with Aquila and Priscilla on his way to the Feast in Jerusalem. He then left them behind to prepare the ground. These two had a profound impact on Apollos, who was already a powerful expositor of the Scriptures, but only knew John's baptism. Through their input, Apollos received mighty new revelation concerning Jesus and the Kingdom and became a powerful preacher of the Kingdom in Corinth. He refuted the Jews, publicly showing that Jesus was indeed the Christ.

When Paul returned some months later, he also found a group of John's disciples who were praying. They had already been baptized with John's baptism of repentance, but they had no power when they prayed. They had been told to believe in Jesus, but they had no revelation of who Jesus really was (see Acts 19:1-6). The limitations of knowing only John's baptism, what I call "John the Baptist Christianity" are fully explained in my first book on the Kingdom, *Heaven on Earth.*[2] Many Christians today live in "John the Baptist Christianity."

Step #2: Establish a Kingdom Company Full of the Holy Spirit (Acts 19:2-7)

Paul immediately became aware that this group of John's disciples in Ephesus needed to have their eyes fully opened, to be properly baptized into the name of Jesus, to enter the Kingdom of God, and to receive the Holy Spirit's power. He explained these things to them, then re-baptized them in the name of Jesus and laid his hands on them. The Spirit fell powerfully upon them, and they spoke with tongues and prophesied.

Step #3: Establish a Foundation of Teaching on the Kingdom (Acts 19:8-10)

Now Paul was ready to begin the assault on Ephesus. As usual, he began in the synagogue reasoning and persuading them from the Scriptures about the things concerning the Kingdom of God and Jesus. Some readily responded, but a growing attitude of resistance and opposition developed among the remaining Jews. As a result, Paul withdrew to the school of Tyrannus and taught there on a daily basis for two years. The goal of his teaching would have been to give a full understanding of the Kingdom of God and the power of the risen life of Jesus flowing through us.

Step #4: Expect an Outbreak of Healings, Deliverances, and Miracles (Acts 19:11-20)

At this time a flow of unusual and powerful miracles took place at the hands of Paul. Many were amazingly healed and delivered from demons when handkerchiefs and aprons that had touched Paul's body were laid upon the sick.

The city of Ephesus was thoroughly shaken, and we read that:

Fear fell on them all, and the name of the Lord Jesus was magnified. And many who had believed came confessing and telling their deeds. Also, many of those who had practiced magic brought their books together and burned them in the sight of all.... So the word of the Lord grew mightily and prevailed (Acts 19:17-20).

Let us be very clear about this: Although a wonderful breakthrough had taken place and many glorious things happened there, the city was not yet taken, and it certainly was not yet transformed. The power of the spirit behind Diana was dented, but was not yet overthrown and was not going to give up easily. A long and bitter battle still lay ahead.

THE SPIRIT OF DIANA COUNTERATTACKS

A very serious countermovement arose when a silversmith named Demetrius organized a violent demonstration of craftsmen who made shrines to Diana. Demetrius did this by convincing them that their lucrative trade and the whole economy of the city was being threatened and undermined by the demise of Diana worship through the preaching of Paul.

The cry of this mob was: *"Great is Diana of the Ephesians!"* (Acts 19:28,34). They rushed into the great amphitheater and began to seize some of the Christian leaders. But once again Paul exercised his heavenly authority, and the Roman official brought a judgment in favor of Paul and his friends. He dismissed the assembly, allowing Paul to depart peaceably for Macedonia.

Paul continued his travels in Macedonia and Greece and strengthened the churches. He then felt compelled by the Holy Spirit to be in Jerusalem in time for the Feast of Pentecost, already knowing that it would lead to chains and imprisonment. On his way to Jerusalem, he stopped briefly in Miletus and called for the elders of the church in Ephesus to come to him (see Acts 20). He powerfully exhorted them to shepherd the Church of God over whom the Holy Spirit had made them overseers. He warned them of some very difficult times that lay ahead. They had a tearful parting, knowing that they would not meet again on earth. (See Acts 20:17-38.)

During the following years, other churches were planted out from Ephesus all over Asia. These churches looked to Ephesus as their apostolic center. The main ones were the seven churches of Asia mentioned in the first three chapters of the Book of Revelation.

Paul left Timothy as the apostle in Ephesus to care for these churches, plus many other churches, such as the one at Crete. (Timothy was later joined or replaced by the apostle John, although we don't know exactly when or why.)

PAUL—A WILLING PRISONER OF THE LORD JESUS

In the later chapters of Acts, we read how Paul went voluntarily to Jerusalem knowing what would happen through the many prophecies that had been given. In Jerusalem, he was arrested and, finally, he was taken in chains to answer directly to Caesar in Rome. They had a very eventful journey including a shipwreck (see Acts 27). Paul then spent his last few years in his own rented house with a measure of freedom, but still as a prisoner. Many members of Caesar's household visited him, and some were converted. As a result, a church was planted in Rome right there inside the Praetorium. Paul refers to some of these things while writing to the Philippians to help them to see that these events were clearly God's will (see Phil. 1:7, 13-14, 4:22).

In this way, God was able to invade the very household of Caesar with the Gospel of the Kingdom, plant a church in Caesar's palace, and so begin His preparations for the Kingdom of God to take over the Roman Empire. However, there were several decades of fierce conflict to come before this finally happened.

During this time, severe persecution of Christians began around A.D. 57 under Emperor Nero. It then continued to come in waves over the next few decades, during which time all the known apostles except John were martyred, as were thousands of other Christians. As a result, the churches were without apostolic leadership at this time of great trial. John was cut off from having any contact with the churches, but was kept alive by the hand of God. He ended up as a slave in the salt mines on the Isle of Patmos from A.D. 81 to A.D. 95, during the more subtle persecution of Emperor Domitian.

In the latter years of this trial, John had some amazing visitations from Jesus, which led him to write the Book of Revelation as he was directly commanded around A.D. 92. A short time later, he was inspired to write the Gospel of John, which was followed by his three letters, all written particularly to Ephesus and the related churches in Asia. Copies of these writings were somehow smuggled out of Patmos and began circulating in the church of Ephesus and among the other churches of Asia, and many other places.

A large group of believers in the churches in Asia, especially among the younger generation, were set ablaze by these writings of John—so much so that they began to pray and wage war against the spirit powers. John was so spoken to by the Spirit that in the years A.D. 92 through A.D. 94, he wrote confidently that he would not die in Patmos, but would soon be set free and would see them face to face (see 2 John 1:12; 3 John 1:14).

Suddenly, in A.D. 95, the emperor Domitian was assassinated, and John was released from Patmos. He returned to Ephesus, where he was received with great joy. Almost immediately, with some of the key intercessors, John went into the great temple of Diana and addressed that spirit directly. He spoke a brief command to the spirit, and it immediately fled. The high altar to Diana physically split into many pieces as if a bomb had exploded, and a third of that great temple collapsed in ruins as if struck by an earthquake.

According to Yale University Professor Ramsay MacMullen, who is quoting Eusebius, who in turn quoted Polycarp, an actual eyewitness to these events, John entered the very temple of Artemis (or Diana), stood before the high altar, and commanded this great principality to flee in the mighty name of Jesus, saying:

God…at whose name every idol takes flight and every demon and every unclean power; now let the demon that is here take flight at thy name ….[3]

MacMullen continues:

And while John was saying this, of a sudden the altar of Artemis split in many pieces…and half the temple fell down. Then the assembled Ephesians cried out, "[There is but] one God, [the God] of John!…We are converted, now that we have seen thy marvelous works! Have mercy upon us O God, according to thy will, and save us from our great error!" And some of them lay on their faces and made supplication, others bent their knees and prayed; some tore their clothes and wept, and others tried to take flight."[4]

All over that great city, from the highest officials to the lowest of the people, many came under deep conviction and pleaded to God for mercy. The whole city was converted, and a new cry went up. It was no longer, "Great is Diana the god of the Ephesians!"; the new cry was "Great is the God of John!"

Starting that day, Ephesus became an entirely Christian city and was a powerful apostolic center for the next 200 years. The church at Ephesus rapidly reached out all over the Roman Empire with the good news of Jesus and His Kingdom, their ministry accompanied by mighty signs and wonders. Within 50 years, Diana was no longer worshiped anywhere in the entirety of the Roman Empire. City after city was taken, and every demonic stronghold was cast down so the people instead bowed the knee to Jesus as King and Lord.

If you don't take anything else away from reading this chapter, I urge you to diligently pray and seek the Lord before trying to displace major principalities and powers in high places. Paul was one of the most powerfully anointed of God's chosen apostles, as demonstrated by the fact he wrote the majority of the New Testament. Yet, he paid a heavy price as he learned many lessons about spiritual warfare. He shared the principles of warfare in the Scriptures for us to follow in His footsteps, if we are so called. I admonish you to be wise, to remain in continuous prayer, and to listen to the promptings of the Holy Spirit at all times.

ENDNOTES

1. *Biblesoft's New Exhaustive Strong's Numbers and Concordance with Expanded Greek-Hebrew Dictionary*. CD-ROM. Biblesoft, Inc. and International

Bible Translators, Inc. (© 1994, 2003, 2006), s.v. "Kathidzo" (NT 2523).

2. Alan Vincent, *Heaven on Earth: Releasing the Power of the Kingdom through YOU* (Shippensburg, PA: Destiny Image Publishers, 2008).

3. Ramsay MacMullen, *Christianizing the Roman Empire (A.D. 100-400)* (New Haven, CT: Yale University Press, 1984), 26.

4. Ibid.

CHAPTER 14

THE FOURTH PHASE OF
THE KINGDOM

TO understand how the Kingdom of God will be ushered into the Earth in its fullness, we must look at where we are in God's timetable. In my earlier book *Heaven on Earth,* I described the first three phases by which the Kingdom of God returned to earth during Jesus' ministry.

The first phase began when John the Baptist began to preach about the Kingdom. However, he was not able to produce any actual manifestation of the Kingdom in his lifetime.

The second phase began as John the Baptist completed his role as a forerunner and was followed immediately by Jesus coming and beginning to preach and manifest the Kingdom of God. Once Jesus was anointed, people began to see an actual manifestation of Kingdom power and authority among the Jews. However, at that stage, that power and authority was restricted to Earth so that Jesus was not yet able to cast down the demonic powers in the heavens that still ruled over the city of Jerusalem. That was one great reason why Jesus willingly went to the cross: to not only pay for our sins but, also, to cast down the prince of this world and then return in the much greater power of His resurrection to destroy all of satan's works.

The third phase began on resurrection day, when Jesus declared that He had been given all power and all authority over all things in Heaven and on earth (see Matt 28:18).

He had carefully explained to His disciples at the Last Supper how He, the Father, and the Spirit would come and make their home in the surrendered humanity of His disciples after His ascension. He then commanded them to wait until they were clothed with power and had learned to sit with His Kingdom authority and rule in His name over the heavenly realm as well as the earthly realm. Once the Spirit had come and clothed them with power, they would be able to cast down the demonic principalities over Jerusalem and see many converted as they preached under the convicting power of an open heaven. This began on the Day of Pentecost, and soon thousands were being added to the Church.

THE FOURTH PHASE—THE GOSPEL INVADES THE GENTILE WORLD

The Gospel of the Kingdom spread quickly to many Jewish communities throughout the Roman Empire, but it did not reach the Gentiles for more than a decade. For a while, amongst the Jewish believers, many of the traditions and customs of the Jews were mixed in with the new revelation of Jesus and the Kingdom.

God gave these Jewish believers a time of grace in which to change; He did this because they had to learn many new things. But He did not wait forever. From the moment Jesus was anointed and began to preach, He made it clear that the Kingdom was for all nations and was not restricted to the Jews. Furthermore, the Kingdom could not continue to be bound and restricted by the many unbiblical traditions of Jewish culture and religious orthodoxy.

Today God is showing the same patience. As the full Gospel of the Kingdom impacts some traditional Christian denominations and Messianic Jewish congregations, some continue to live in their familiar traditions. Over the years, most major Christian denominations have created their own complex law-bound traditions in a similar way to what the orthodox Jews did in the days of the early Church. In each case, many of these traditions were unbiblical. While God is patient and extends grace for a time, He will not wait forever.

If we behave like the Jews in David's day, who stayed with the "safer," more familiar tabernacle of Moses after David's tabernacle had been raised up, we risk missing the power and the authority that God has for us, just as they missed it in their day. It may be a bit scary to move into the new thing that God is doing, but His unfettered Kingdom has the power to change our cities so that, at last, the will of God will begin to be done on earth, in secular society, as it is in Heaven.

Let's now look more carefully at the fourth phase of the Kingdom. All over the world right now, there has been a developing manifestation of the Kingdom with growing understanding of how to exercise spiritual authority and power in the heavenly realm. However, it is being hampered by various doctrinal positions and church traditions that have restricted the full flow of its power.

In the early Church, the Jewish traditions hindered the full power of the Kingdom from being manifested in society. The particulars of those traditions are not important for us to consider right now. Rather, I want to concentrate more on the underlying principle. As the power of the Kingdom began to move into the Gentile world, Jewish traditions prevented new believers from entering the fullness of freedom that is part of God's Kingdom. Although Jesus did not shake everything at once, but instead allowed a period of grace for people to make the change, change *was* required.

These traditions, with their multitudes of rules and regulations, were largely derived from the Talmud, or the oral law of the Jews. These traditions bound orthodox Jews in a myriad of regulations regarding dress, external behavior, and eating habits. They also strongly suppressed women. Most of these rules were not written by Moses or the prophets or recorded in the Torah or the Tanakh (which comprised the 24 books of the complete Jewish Old Testament). The majority of these demands were not found in the actual written Scriptures.

These rules were allegedly extrapolated from those Scriptures, but over the centuries, their interpretation gradually became more and more distorted. Many new rules that God never intended were added by legalistic scribes as they passed from one generation to the next. This oral tradition was later written down in a book called the Talmud. One version originated in Constantinople, and another version came from Babylon.

The Talmud was the only book that many sincere Jews read because only a very few Jews owned an actual written copy of the original Scriptures. There was usually only one copy of these Holy Scriptures in every community, which was kept in the local synagogue and was read only by the priests. It was written in Hebrew, which the majority of Jews no longer understood. But the Talmud was more widely available in book form and was available in Greek.

Gradually these myriad regulations got further and further from the original Scriptures and what they actually said. After many generations, the rules of the Talmud were wrongly taught by the priests as having more authority and relevance to ordinary, devout Jews than the Scriptures themselves. People were taught to obey the Talmud and what the priests said it meant. The priests discouraged the ordinary people from trying to read what the actual Scriptures said because they were considered too difficult for "ordinary" people to understand.

A similar process occurred in a number of historic Christian denominations. If the Bible was read at all, it was usually read in Greek or Latin, languages which had become dead in certain cultures and which few people understood. The Christian orthodox priests taught that the Scriptures were too difficult for "ordinary" people to understand, and they were discouraged from reading them. Instead, they were taught to believe and obey what the priests told them about Scripture.

Where there was an apparent contradiction between the original Scriptures and what the Church taught through its priests, the Church leaders determined that the teaching of the "church" through its priests was to have the final authority.

This was how John Wycliffe, John Huss, Martin Luther, and others got into trouble as they became ardent students of the original Greek New Testament manuscripts. They found that some of the great truths of Scripture had been set aside by the traditions of the Church. This led to a great battle for truth, which ultimately led to the great Reformation breaking forth in many parts of Europe during the late 15th and early 16th centuries.

In a similar way, during the life of Jesus until well after the days when the Church was born, the words of the Talmud were quoted much more frequently than the original Scriptures. In Jesus' day, the actual Torah or Tanakh was rarely read except in the synagogue on the Sabbath. A number of important prophetic passages, such as Isaiah 53 and Isaiah 61:1-9, concerning the coming of Messiah were deliberately omitted from these daily readings for two reasons: They were considered too hard to understand, and there was a doctrinal battle between the Pharisees and scribes on the one hand and the Essenes on the other.[1]

Jesus said to the scribes and Pharisees, *"All too well you reject the commandment of God, that you may keep your tradition"*(Mark 7:9). On another occasion He said, *"You are mistaken, not knowing the Scriptures..."*(Matt. 22:29).

The Essenes had an eager expectation in Jesus' day that the Messiah would soon come, but they saw it only in political terms. They believed He was some-one who would come and deliver them from Roman rule and set up another political kingdom, as happened in David's day. As a result, they were more responsive to Jesus and His teachings, but for the wrong reason. The scribes and the Pharisees, on the other hand, generally suppressed this teaching because they feared it would get them into trouble with the Roman authorities.

WOMEN GO FREE

When the Church began, women did not come into their full role alongside the men for several decades. So much of what was written in the Talmud kept women nonfunctional and bound in silence and passivity. But these restrictions were not written in the Torah (the actual inspired Old Testament Scriptures). Women were placed in a false prison invented by religious and chauvinistic men.

Within a couple of decades of the birth of the Church, some Christian religious leaders were hard at work weaving a similar web of rules and regulations allegedly extrapolated from the Scriptures to bind Christians in a similar way. Paul vigorously resisted every manifestation of this kind and commanded Jew and Gentile believers alike to stand fast in the liberty in which Christ had set them free, but without ever using that liberty as an excuse for the flesh (see Gal. 5:1,13).

Like almost all evangelical Christians of my day, when Eileen, my wife, and I were converted in 1958, we were brought up spiritually under this kind of well-meaning Christian evangelical legalism. After a few years, we began to see things differently, and with my encouragement, Eileen started her gradual move toward liberty.

Before that, she was a head-covering, Brethren lady who kept absolutely quiet in the church, and like all the other women, did not actively participate. We both have come a long way since those days as God liberated us from those restrictive traditions and set us free. I eventually came to the place where I could accept women functioning in leadership, eldership, and even as Ephesians 4:11 ministries. I could also see that a man and his wife could be in an apostolic partnership together. This was the way that Eileen and I had so obviously been called to function, just like Priscilla and Aquila did in Scripture.

The Scriptures also mention a woman named Junia, who is described as being *"of note among the apostles"* (Rom. 16:7). She could have been a single apostle in her own right; or as some have suggested, she could have been married to Andronicus who is mentioned alongside her in the same verse, although with no scriptural indication that they were married (see Rom. 16:7).

For years, even after I had accepted the reality of present-day apostles, I continued to teach that apostolic ministry was a man's ministry because it was a fathering, governmental ministry that women could not do. One of my main arguments was that if Jesus had wanted women to be apostles, then surely He would have appointed at least one woman in the original 12 and so make a point that we would all understand.

Many years ago, I was asked to pray at a large conference over a well-known couple where the woman, particularly, was being used in a powerful international ministry. As I laid my hands on both of them, I felt compelled to prophesy, especially to the woman. To my surprise and dismay, I heard myself confirming her clearly as an apostle and telling her from God that she was to carry that office boldly without fear or apology. I was shocked because I did not even believe in what I was saying at the time. But I knew in my spirit that I had spoken the truth by the Spirit of God, in spite of the doctrinal position that I then held.

So I went before God and said, "Lord, I know that as I prophesied I spoke the truth. But I'm not able to prove that what I said was scripturally accurate. Please give me some biblical proof because I know people will be calling me and wanting to meet with me. Some are going to attack me, and they will eat me alive unless I can prove this from Scripture."

Then I asked God, "Why didn't You appoint a woman as one of the 12 apostles? Then we would all know." He said to me, "Alan, if I had made a woman one of the original 12 apostles, the Jewish culture at that time was so prejudiced against women that they would not have allowed her to function. I had to break the bondage of those Jewish traditions before I could bring the Kingdom to its full power and liberty."

God said, "Look at Junia, a woman who was an apostle."

I replied, "But she was married to Andronicus, and he gave her covering."

God said, "Does it really say that?" Of course, it doesn't. So I started to read the Bible more carefully and also read some of the writings of the early Church fathers more fully. I discovered that within a few decades, women were moving in all the Ephesians 4:11 ministries with great power and authority, including the apostolic.

Let me qualify this before we leave this subject. Although in Christ there is neither male nor female in terms of worth and value and inheritance before God, in this life there is still a difference in the nature and function of men and women. I still believe that men are called to be fathers and that women are called to be mothers in the family and in the Church. Both have governmental authority, but their roles are different and not totally interchangeable. I do not believe in genderless parenting, naturally or spiritually. Both men and women bring the uniqueness of their gender into these shepherding and caring situations. There are differences between how men function in apostolic ministry and how women function in apostolic ministry.

In the same way, men will function in eldership in a different way from women. The function of fathering in churches is still a man's role, as it is in the natural family. But there are all sorts of ways in which women can function apostolically in the establishing, building, and development of churches without trying to be apostolic fathers.

This is just one example of the need to break out from our stereotypes and traditions that hinder the Kingdom's advance. There were many other restrictions and handicaps on the freedom of the Kingdom while it remained within the boundaries of Jewish tradition, and they had to be broken, not only for the sake of the Gentiles, but also for the sake of the Jews themselves.

DON'T FORSAKE GOD'S WORD FOR TRADITIONS

Jesus strongly rebuked the Pharisees and the scribes for setting aside the Word of God for their traditions. We must be careful not to do the same thing.

All of this drove me into a new, prayerful study of some of the things I had believed and had been teaching for years. I began to see that I needed to change some of my own mindsets. It may not be Jewish tradition that is hindering many of us. It could be Catholic tradition, Episcopalian tradition, Pentecostal tradition, Baptist tradition, Brethren tradition, Holiness tradition, Classical Reformed Theology tradition, or even some more recent things like the Vineyard Movement, the Discipleship Movement, or the Word of Faith Movement.

It's amazing how quickly these new movements develop their own traditions and rules, which are extrapolated from Scripture rather than being the balanced, real truth of the Word of God. If we are not careful, they can bind us so we are not free to simply respond to God and His Word as He shows us new things.

These various denominations and movements were all valuable and helped us to take several new steps in the right direction, but none of them were the full revelation. We need to recognize that some of us have carried a lot of baggage into the Kingdom from our past, and it can restrict and dilute the full freedom and power of the Kingdom flowing through us.

As David came to the throne in the Old Testament, his kingdom did not really come with power until the tabernacle of David was fully set up and properly established. This could not happen until a lot of the deduced rules of Moses' Law and Jewish traditions were abandoned.

David's tent was free from all the rules and practice of Moses' Law and Jewish tradition. Never was a sin offering made, as required in Moses' law and Jewish tradition. King David, though not a priest himself, nor of the tribe of Levi, but of the tribe of Judah, freely entered into the presence of God. In fact, the glorious freedom of David's tent was demonstrated by laymen and priests together worshipping and praying before the ark of the covenant without penalty of death. (See 2 Sam. 6:17-18; 1 Chron. 16.) Melchizedek, Jesus Christ Himself, was the High Priest of David's tabernacle, just as He is also the only High Priest of the New Covenant and of the Kingdom of God. (See Heb. 7:1-3, 14-17.)

In David's tabernacle there were no complex religious rules and regulations to obey, just a few basic biblical requirements of purity, holiness, integrity, and humility linked to a passionate devotion to God and His will. In David's tabernacle, which was for those who would pay the price of intimacy with God, everybody enjoyed unveiled, face-to-face fellowship with almighty God in the person of Melchizedek.

Apart from those things, they were free from many religious restrictions; but motivated by love, they disciplined themselves to live only to please Him and do whatever He told them to do. Their passion was to advance His Kingdom and glorify His name among the nations.

The liberty that came into the emerging Church was initially forced upon them by the Gentiles as they began to pour into the Church. The Gentiles knew nothing of the Jewish religion or its traditions. They did not cut their hair the traditional Jewish way. They did not wear special clothes to come to meetings with religious, pious looks on their faces.

Instead, they probably had long hair, strange clothes, earrings, and all kinds of jewelry. But they were totally excited about Jesus and passionate about loving Him and serving Him with all their hearts. They were completely committed to forcefully advancing His Kingdom and were much more able to communicate effectively with the lost people all around them. This caused an immediate negative reaction from the traditional Jews, which brought about the first Council of Jerusalem recorded in Acts 15:1-21.

After hearing the various points of view and then praying to hear from God, James was led by the Spirit to the promise of God in Amos 9:11-12. The promise was that in the last days, God would raise again the tabernacle of David which had fallen down, and rebuild its ruins, so that *the rest of humankind* would seek the Lord, especially all the Gentiles who are called by His name.

As a result, James brought a judgment freeing the new Gentile believers from any need to be circumcised or obey the traditions of Moses' law in any way. They were released entirely from these traditions and were soon followed by many Jews, who also abandoned their traditions and rejoiced in their newfound liberty in Christ.

Once we come into Christ's Kingdom, there is no longer Jew or Greek, male or female, rich or poor, slave or free—it is not any of these things, but one new creation! (See 2 Cor. 5:17; Gal. 3:27-28, 6:15.)

The raising of David's tabernacle included total abandonment in praise and worship to Jesus, but it required much more than that. It was also necessary to become totally released from any former religious, worldly, or pagan traditions, whatever they may have been. Within the early Church, Jewish tradition was the stumbling block to so many. But today it could be one of the many religious or cultural traditional backgrounds from which we have come.

With these basic Kingdom requirements—love and intimacy with the Father, radical holiness of life, and total obedience to whatever He commanded the early Christians to do—and the power of the Holy Spirit manifested in signs, wonders, and miracles, the Kingdom was ready to take Europe. It soon swept through city after city, and the whole of the continent of Europe was rapidly and dramatically impacted by the Kingdom of God.

Today, so much of what was abandoned by the early Church has been put back in the form of religious traditions. We must break out again and raise the tabernacle of David. When it is fully raised up and properly repaired, it will be the power that transforms our cities, our nation, and other nations of the world.

We must be prepared to pay a price to restore the tabernacle of David in our day.

First, it requires a total abandonment of ourselves to God in extravagant love and worship, which operates in our spirits, souls, and bodies.

Second, we must come to new, higher standards of purity, truth, humility, and holiness that are compatible with God so that we can live comfortably in His awesome presence.

Third, there must be a deep relationship with God where He is intimately known as Father in a personal way so we, like David and his mighty men and even more so Jesus, can clearly hear His voice.

Fourth, there must be total childlike obedience to His will so that we do whatever He tells us to do without question.

When the early Church moved into that fourth dimension of the Kingdom, nothing could stand in their way. They first saw certain key cities transformed and then whole nations. Entire continents were powerfully impacted in a few short years. They sacrificed everything and gained the Kingdom. I believe that as we move into the final stages of the fourth dimension, we are going to see even greater impact and advancement of the Kingdom in our day.

ENDNOTE

1. The Essenes were a zealous, militant religious sect within the Jewish nation. They came to greater fame with the discovery of the Dead Sea scrolls.

CHAPTER 15

TIME FOR NEW WINE AND
A NEW WINESKIN

IN each of the three synoptic Gospels, several chapters are devoted to the teaching of Jesus on the "new wine" and the "new wineskin" (see Luke 5:36-39; Mark 2:18-22; Matt. 9:15-17). There is a lot of repetition and overlap, but each record adds some extra, important detail. We will follow this important subject mainly from Luke's Gospel, which is also the only place in Scripture where we get precious glimpses of the boyhood years of Jesus.

THIRTY YEARS OF WAITING

To fulfill all righteousness and be the perfect Savior of both Jew and Gentile, Jesus was born under the law and had to fulfill all the just requirements of the law. In His deity, He is and was the only Eternal Son of God. As a Man, all the fullness of the Godhead dwelt bodily in Him (see Col. 2:9). Nevertheless, to qualify as God's Son in His humanity, it was necessary for Him to live His first 30 years in perfect obedience to the Father. In this way, He qualified to become the first and only human Son of God (see Gal. 4:4-5).

At the age of 30 years, like every Jewish man, Jesus came into His inheritance. But He was God's only begotten Son, so when His 30 years of obedience were complete, He was able to come into His inheritance as the Son of Man with a mature Son's rights of access to all the treasure and resources of His Father. Also, as the Son of Man He would be able to use these resources legally, on earth and against the devil. In this way, He would destroy the devil and remove his whole kingdom of darkness from the earth.

Until that 30th birthday came, Jesus could only wait and watch satan's terrible activity on Earth and was not able to do anything about it. He prepared Himself in advance by avidly studying the Scriptures and by maintaining a deep intimacy with His heavenly Father. He also learned to be subject to Joseph and Mary until the time of His release (see Luke 2:42-52).

JESUS THE CARPENTER

Jesus became a skilled carpenter under the tutelage of Joseph, his earthly father, and for many years worked diligently in His trade while biding His time. On one of the family visits to Jerusalem, He probably went through the ceremony of a Bar Mitzvah and became "a son of the law." He was then free to attend the local synagogue every Sabbath with his family and sit with the men and take part in its life and traditions, including reading aloud the set reading of Scripture (see Luke 4:14-16). He would then be expected to keep all the commandments of the law.

At some point, Joseph died. We are not told exactly when that was, but it was not before Mary had given birth to four other sons and several daughters in the usual, natural way as Joseph's wife (see Matt. 1:24-25; Mark 6:3). We know that Joseph was in Jerusalem with Jesus at the Feast of Passover when Jesus was 12 years old (see Luke 2:42), so we can safely conclude that Jesus must have been a teenager before Joseph died.

Jesus then took the full responsibilities of the eldest son and cared for his mother and worked hard as a carpenter to provide for their large family. He was well known in the town of Nazareth, but only as Jesus, the carpenter. In the synagogue meeting, He would often stand to indicate His desire to read the set Scripture for that day. I'm sure it must have been a wonderful experience to all who attended that synagogue to hear Jesus read those precious words.

During those years Jesus complied with all the traditions and rules of orthodox Jewish life and was a model Jewish young Man in every way. He did nothing to rock the boat because His time had not yet come. It was not time for any changes to "the wineskin," that is, the structure and traditions of the way they practiced their Jewish religion, because the "new wine" had to come first. The "new wine" was the way Jesus described the power and manifestation of the Holy Spirit.

TEMPTED BY THE DEVIL

At last! Knowing the spiritual significance of His 30th birthday, Jesus willingly went down to the Jordan to join the large crowd waiting to be baptized by John the Baptist. When His turn came, John protested and said it ought to be the other way around: Jesus should be baptizing him. But Jesus said, *"Permit it to be so now, for thus it is fitting for us to fulfill all righteousness"* (Matt. 3:15). John agreed; as Jesus went down into the water to be baptized, the Holy Spirit descended upon Him in the form of a dove. The voice of the Father spoke from Heaven and said, *"This is My beloved Son in whom I am well pleased"* (Matt. 3:17).

We are then told that Jesus, *"being filled with the Holy Spirit"* (Luke 4:1), immediately went into the wilderness to be tested or tempted by the devil. To begin to comprehend these temptations and their purpose, we must understand that Jesus, as a Man, had to live every moment of His human life by faith in what the Spirit of God was showing to His human spirit. The Spirit was also giving Him a full revelation of what each page of the written Old Testament Scriptures really meant.

At some point as He was growing up, it must have gradually been made clear to Jesus by the Spirit that He was the Messiah or the Christ that the prophetic

Scriptures had spoken about so powerfully for hundreds of years. But He only knew this by faith and through the revelation of the Word and the Spirit to His human spirit. We are told that He was sorely tempted in every way, just as we are, but He never gave in to those temptations and doubts and never wavered in His faith. As a result of His amazing faith, He remained without sin (see Heb. 4:15).

At the moment of His water baptism, when God joyfully and with a loud voice declared from Heaven to the watching crowd who Jesus really was, Jesus the man was recognized as God's first Man with all the rights of His mature Sonship. He now had full legal access to all of His inheritance; the implications of this must have sent great shock waves throughout the realm of darkness. Little did they know that Jesus was but the first and the beginning of a whole new race, a God-chosen generation (see 1 Pet. 2:9). For the first time since the fall of Adam, a Man was now established on earth with the legal right to rule as God's delegated authority. As a Man, He could now move on the earth with all the power and resources of God's Kingdom freely available to Him. He was armed with a warring faith to fulfill His declared purpose, which was to take back everything on earth from the devil and completely destroy his kingdom and all his works.

This joyful declaration by the Father proclaimed that He now had a human Son on Earth whom He had legally clothed with power. His words spelled destruction to the entire kingdom of darkness. Knowing that these vast Kingdom resources could only be accessed and then released on earth by the Man's faith, satan's tactic was to try to get Jesus to doubt who He was and what He could do. It was the devil's only hope to thwart God's great plan to redeem the whole earth and save fallen humankind.

It would take far too long in this book to fully examine the subtle way in which each temptation was crafted by the devil to sow doubt into Jesus' heart. Suffice it to say that each was based on Jesus' experiences and circumstances and was designed, as already mentioned, to question the reality of His Sonship. Satan began every temptation with the words: *"If you are the Son of God…."* Each time, Jesus simply replied with the words: *"It is written…."* (See Matthew 4; Luke 4.)

Jesus was far too strong for the devil and too resistant to every temptation. He refused to be moved off the solid rock of God's Word onto the sinking sands of feelings, circumstance, or experience.

The devil finally left Him in defeat. *"Jesus returned* [from the wilderness] *in the power of the Spirit..."* (Luke 4:14). Jesus then immediately stepped out and began His miraculous ministry at a wedding in Cana, which is recorded in John 2:1-11.

JESUS' FIRST MIRACLE—WATER INTO WINE

Mary, Jesus, and His disciples were guests at a wedding in Cana of Galilee. The wine for the guests was running low, so in the midst of this perceived crisis, Mary tried to push Jesus into doing things in the wrong order. He told her that His time had not yet come, but she knew that whatever He spoke would be fulfilled.

At this time John the Baptist was still free, teaching and baptizing. Jesus knew that He had to wait until John had finished his course before He began to preach His Kingdom message and demonstrate the power of that Kingdom (see John 3:24). So Jesus responded to His mother by saying, "My time has not yet come" (see John 2:4) Nevertheless, He decided to demonstrate a miracle by turning the water into wine. This first miracle was instrumental in building His disciples' faith.

ABUNDANT NEW WINE—AN ALLEGORICAL PICTURE

The abundance of the new wine produced by this miracle was a picture of the abundance of the power of God flowing out through the eternal life of Jesus. It would now begin to flow out like a great river to bless, deliver, and save multitudes; it would then go on to mend their individual relationships with the Father so they could know Him, love Him, and serve Him as Jesus did.

Jesus decided to make this first miracle, which took place at a wedding feast, an allegory of the Church. Although the Church did not exist yet, He knew it would soon come forth. In other Scriptures concerning the Church, she is pictured as a glorious Bride without spot, blemish, wrinkle, or any such thing, and she will be presented to Jesus like this at the end of this age (see Eph. 5:27).

This new wine was going to totally replace all ceremonial religion, even amongst the Jews. The ceremonial water in the rigid stone pots represented the Jewish religious law, and the stone pots represented its inflexible rules and regulations. These rules concentrated on the external appearance and not on the internal condition of the heart. All this religion and law-keeping was going to be turned miraculously into the good new wine of the Spirit. It was going to be much better than the old wine!

ABUNDANCE OF PROVISION

The six water pots held about 20 to 30 gallons of water apiece. That meant that this water became about 120 to 180 gallons of fantastic new wine! It would be equivalent to about 1,000 present-day bottles of good, new wine. This was an enormous amount of wine for any wedding party. Remember, they had already drunk plenty of the old!

THREE BARRIERS TO THE NEW WINE

Because of rules, regulations, and mindsets, the new wine would be resisted by many. Three main things stood in the way:

1. The law-bound legalism of Judaism, particularly as expressed by the Pharisees and scribes, focused on outward behavior and centered around many rules and regulations concerning dress, washing, eating, and drinking—not at all on the condition of the heart.

2. The rationalism and liberalism of the Sadducees prevented their believing what they could not intellectually understand or explain. Therefore, they rejected anything and everything miraculous, even the miracles that were recorded in the Old Testament Scriptures.

3. The disciples of John the Baptist already believed themselves to be on the cutting edge of the new thing that God was doing. Because it was new, they had paid a price to get there. They at first resisted the new wine that Jesus brought, thinking that the "older wine" they were drinking was the best.

NEW LIFE—NOT REFURBISHED WINESKINS.

The new wine, or the new life of the Spirit, must come first. Trying to change the old order or the old wineskin too soon before the new wine has come only causes disputes. It does not bring life. If you try to bring change by a new method or superior arguments before the new wine has come, you just cause strong counterarguments to be put forth. This leads to fights, bitterness, splits, and division. That's why Jesus never tried to change the traditions in His family's local synagogue.

There have been a number of significant movements amongst Christians in the last few decades; many of them have originated in the United States and/or North America. For example, since 1960s we have had: the Charismatic Movement, the Discipleship Movement, the Word of Faith Movement, the Toronto Blessing Revival, and the Brownsville Revival. In addition, there have been a number of other outbreaks in other parts of the world, including South Korea, Central and South America, Fiji, Indonesia, and parts of Africa and India.

Each movement had some valuable new things to contribute to the Body of Christ. They were steps in the right direction, but they were not complete. In the places where they first broke out, they initially had life in them. But as each one was copied, codified, and exported as a methodology to other parts of the world, it lacked the original life that drove its beginnings. The move was soon strangled. The inflexible, old wineskin could not change to accommodate the new wine, so both the wine and the wineskin were spoiled (see Luke 5:37).

In Jesus' time, the Sadducees and Pharisees were always fighting each other about some doctrinal issue such as the reality of angelic visitations, the belief in literal miracles of the past, and the reality of people being raised from the dead. Also, John the Baptist's disciples soon got into arguments about fasting and Jewish purification rites with the disciples of Jesus (see Luke 5:33; John 3:25-30).

FINDING THE TRUTH

The new wine itself prepared the way for the new wineskin to be joyfully received by those who were of the truth. Jesus said that once the new wine had come, sooner or later all those who were of the truth would come and drink of the new wine. If they have already tasted the old wine, they might at first say the old is better, but eventually they would accept the new wine because the Holy Spirit would draw them and show them the truth.

NICODEMUS CAME

Nicodemus, a Pharisee and ruler of the Jews, was one of the greatest Bible teachers of his day. He was not immediately convinced by the teaching of Jesus, because Jesus' words shook so much of his theology. Nicodemus was, however, convinced by the life that Jesus manifested and by the miracles he saw Jesus do. These signs opened his heart to the message of the Kingdom, and he said to Jesus, "...*no one can do these signs that You do unless God is with him*" (John 3:2).

Once the new wine began to flow, as Jesus had promised, all those who were of the truth began to come to Him. They came from various backgrounds, including some Sadducees, Pharisees, and disciples of John the Baptist; and they soon became united in the one new thing God was doing. They forgot their original identities and their formerly irresolvable differences and arguments. They were able to become a united community and one Body in the Spirit through the power of the new wine.

TIMING OF THE NEW WINE TRANSITION

Until the new wine came, Jesus never violated the religious rules. For 18 years after He had become a Bar Mitzvah, Jesus was perfectly compliant to all the traditions of His culture and His religious upbringing. But when the new wine came, He immediately began to dismantle all unbiblical traditions (many of which were based on the Talmud) because they seriously hindered the flow of this new wine.

He tore down the non-biblical traditions and rules, which had been added by generations of scribes and Pharisees. The old wineskin now had to go—completely. This included many human-made rules, such as those regarding the Sabbath. Jesus declared: *"The Sabbath was made for man, and not man for the Sabbath. Therefore the Son of Man is also Lord of the Sabbath"* (Mark 2:27-28).

NEW WINE DEMANDS A NEW WINESKIN

A wineskin was still needed, but it had to be a different one. New wine could not be allowed to flow all over the place, uncontrolled and without boundaries. Without a new wineskin, the new wine would have been lost. It had to be contained. But this new wineskin also had to be flexible and gentle so as to contain the new wine without overly restricting it or putting it under excessive pressure. Otherwise, the new wine would burst the skin and destroy everything. The Holy Spirit must be listened to continuously, obeyed very carefully, and allowed to form this new, absolutely biblical, flexible container, as He directs. This is accomplished through the revelation of His Word to His apostolic leaders.

NEW WINE REACHES THE JEWS IN NAZARETH.

Jesus returned in the power of the Spirit, after a short time in Capernaum and Cana, to His own hometown of Nazareth on the Sabbath. It was the Sabbath that began the Feast of Trumpets, a festival leading immediately into the Feast of Tabernacles. On that very day, He entered the synagogue and stood up to read.

The scroll of Scriptures was then handed to Him, probably already opened at the traditional place for the set reading for that day, which was Isaiah chapter 61 beginning at verse 10. But, Jesus did not start to read from verse 10, instead He rolled back the scroll and began to read from verse 1.

According to the tradition of the scribes and Pharisees, Isaiah 61 verses 1 through 9 were never to be read in the synagogue; they were taught that these verses would one day be read by the Messiah Himself when He came. So Jesus deliberately violated this tradition and began reading. His words are recorded in Luke's Gospel:

> The Spirit of the LORD is upon Me, because He has anointed Me to preach the gospel to the poor; He has sent Me to heal the brokenhearted, to proclaim liberty to the captives and recovery of sight to the blind, to set at liberty those who are oppressed; to proclaim the acceptable year of the LORD (Luke 4:18-19).

The passage Jesus quoted reads as follows:

> The Spirit of the LORD God is upon Me, because the LORD has anointed Me to preach good tidings to the poor; He has sent Me to heal the brokenhearted, to proclaim liberty to the captives, and the opening of the prison to those who are bound; to proclaim the acceptable year of the LORD, and the day of vengeance of our God... (Isa. 61:1-2)

At this point, Jesus closed the scroll, sat down, and then very deliberately said, *"**Today** this Scripture has been fulfilled in your hearing"* (Luke 4:21 NASB), thus declaring Himself to be the Messiah.

You can imagine the shocked response in that synagogue. They were immediately faced with a huge decision: Either Jesus had spoken the truth, in which case they should fall down and worship Him, or He was blaspheming and deserved to be stoned.

The response of the majority was immediate and violent. In furious opposition, they rushed at Him; they pushed Him out of the synagogue and out of the city toward a nearby cliff. They intended to push Him over the cliff and kill Him, but Jesus supernaturally passed through their midst and went on His way (see Luke 4:28-30).

Jesus responded by becoming even more violent in the Spirit when dealing with the scribes and Pharisees. He let loose a mighty flow of new wine in the form of many miracles to confirm His words. These miracles had a great impact on the surrounding regions and nations.

In Matthew 4:23-25 we read:

> And Jesus went about all Galilee, teaching in their synagogues, preaching the gospel of the kingdom, and healing all kinds of sickness and all kinds of disease among the people. Then His fame went throughout all Syria; and they brought to Him all sick people who were afflicted with various diseases and torments, and those who were demon-possessed, epileptics, and paralytics; and He healed them. Great multitudes followed Him—from Galilee, and from Decapolis, Jerusalem, Judea, and beyond the Jordan.

He immediately began to dismantle all the traditions which stood in the way of the new wine. For example, in His first major teaching after these events (usually called The Sermon on the Mount), Jesus set in place many of the foundational principles of living in the Kingdom. This teaching is most fully recorded in Matthew 5:1–7:29.

Jesus began with nine basic "be-attitudes," which in the Kingdom must become the real attitudes of our hearts (see Matt. 5:3-12).

Jesus then took six of the basic teachings of Moses' Law and reinterpreted them; in so doing, He took them to totally new heights, showing that our actions must be motivated by a transformed heart and not be a mere outward show. He made it quite clear that He had not come to destroy the law, but to fulfill it by taking it to a much higher level (see Matt. 5:17).

He also stated plainly that unless our righteousness exceeded the righteousness of the scribes and the Pharisees, we would in no way be able to enter the Kingdom of Heaven (see Matt. 5:20). He said anyone who teaches a lower standard would be least in the Kingdom of Heaven. He dealt with temper and anger, sexual purity, lust, adultery, divorce and remarriage, the keeping of promises, the importance of being people of truth who keep their word, the sinfulness of revenge, and the godliness of forgiveness. (See Matthew 5:17-48.)

There has been a tendency amongst many sections of the Church in recent times to lower the standards of righteousness in many of these areas, using the excuse that we are not under law, but under grace. However, the New Testament clearly teaches us that the grace of God is not given to lower the standard of our righteousness; it is given to supernaturally empower us and take us to a level not reachable through human effort in keeping the Jewish law or any other set of religious rules.

By the power of the risen life of Jesus imparted to us by the indwelling Holy Spirit as a free gift of grace, we can now live above the law. We don't abandon the law with its many good and righteous principles; we surpass the law in the new freedom and power of the Kingdom of God.

I remember a little rhyme from years ago which said:

"Do this and live" the Law demands,

but gives me neither hands nor feet.

But a better hope the Gospel brings.

It bids me, "Fly!"

but it gives me wings.

Hallelujah! In the power of the Spirit and the flow of the new wine, the flow of miracles really began and multitudes came to Him. Many were healed and many demons were cast out (see Luke 4:31-6:19, 7:1-15, 8:22-56).

These three important principles were clearly given to us by Jesus:

1. The new wine must come first before the new wineskin can be formed.

2. The old wineskin is removed and replaced by a suitable new wineskin, which is flexible and able to move with the Spirit. Yet, this new wineskin must be able to gently contain the new wine and never allow it to break out in a disorderly and destructive way.

3. Once the new wine has come, no part of the old wineskin can be allowed to remain. Otherwise, both the new wine and the old wineskin will be spoiled.

JESUS' PRAYER LIFE—NEW WINE'S DRIVING FORCE

Luke particularly focuses on the prayer life of Jesus. We can learn many valuable lessons by studying these passages of Scripture and imitating Jesus in His prayer life as He has commanded us.

These principles were fully taught in my book *The Good Fight of Faith.*[1] The following is an outline of that teaching:

1. Luke 3:21-22: As Jesus was praying, the heavens opened and the Spirit descended upon Him.

2. Luke 4:40-44: Jesus healed the sick and cast out many demons. He went into a desert place and fasted and prayed to maintain the flow of power.

3. Luke 5:16-17: Jesus often withdrew into the wilderness and prayed. As a result, the power of the Lord was continually present to heal them.

4. Luke 6:12-13,19: Jesus continued all night in prayer and afterward chose the 12 disciples. When believing people touched Him, power went out from Him to heal them all.

5. Luke 8:46: Because Jesus prayed, power went out from Him and healed the woman's issue of blood.

6. Luke 9:18-20: As Jesus was praying, some of His disciples joined Him and, by divine revelation, Peter was able to see who Jesus really was.

7. Luke 11:1-22: By the example of His prayer life, one of His disciples was moved to ask Him to teach them to pray. He taught them five steps to powerful praying which would finally give them the authority to bind the strong man and rob him of all his goods. This proved that the Kingdom of God was more powerful than any strong man.

8. Luke 11:20: Through his powerful personal prayer life, Jesus was able to cast out demons *with the finger of God....*"This was the sure sign that the Kingdom of God had truly come.

9. Luke 22:39-46: By agonizing intercessory prayer, Jesus obtained His resurrection as a fact of faith in the Garden of

Gethsemane even before He went to the cross. (See also Heb. 5:7.)

10. Luke 23:34-46: By His amazing prayer of faith, even while on the cross, Jesus obtained mighty answers from His intercession and robbed the devil of all his goods. (See also Matt. 27:46-53; Ps. 22.)

"THE TWELVE," "THE SEVENTY," AND THE NEW WINE

Jesus sent out a group of 12 disciples and a group of 70 with the new wine (see Matt. 10:5-15; Luke 10:1-12). They went out as apostolic delegates of Jesus. As they went out, they were empowered spiritually by the power of His prayer life, by His anointing, and by His power being imparted to them. It was His prayer life, His anointing, and His faith that fueled their ministry and made it effective as He spiritually flowed through them.

He first sent out the 12 expressly to the lost sheep of the house of Israel and forbade them to go to the Gentiles or Samaritans. Then in Luke chapter 10 we read that Jesus sent out the 70 as apostolic delegates.

This time they were not restricted and went two-by-two to every place that Jesus was about to go. They returned with great joy because even the demons were subject to them. Jesus gave them authority and power over the enemy, promising them that nothing would by any means hurt them (see Luke 10:19). At this Jesus rejoiced in the Spirit and *"saw Satan fall like lightning from heaven"* (Luke 10:18).

THE NEW WINE: MANIFESTATION OF THE KINGDOM

Until the new wine comes, Kingdom talk is only theory; but when the new wine actually comes, everybody can see the Kingdom and its authority as demons are cast out, sicknesses and diseases are healed, and many are added to the Kingdom.

In Matthew 9:35-38 we read of Jesus' compassion for the multitude and of His prayer for more laborers. Although multitudes came to Him and were being wonderfully healed, Jesus saw they had many other needs that only patient, loving, pastoral shepherding could cure. He longed to make them whole in every way and prayed for laborers to be quickly released into this great harvest waiting to be reaped.

Notwithstanding all the healings and miracles, Jesus longed for the full flow of the Kingdom to begin; He was eager for that day to come when He would send fire upon the earth. For that to happen, He knew He had to go to Calvary and be baptized with the redemptive suffering of crucifixion, followed by the resurrection power of the cross. (See Luke 12:49-56.)

Jesus longed for the cross because He knew the full manifestation of the Kingdom could not happen until then. The cross, the resurrection, and the Pentecostal outpouring opened the way for the full flow of the new wine to come. Then, after He was risen, Jesus, the Spirit, and the Father could actually be *in* these disciples and not just *with* them (see John 14:10–16:28). They would be able to do His works in even greater measure because Jesus could be His risen fullness in them and through them.

The Spirit, however, still had to come to the apostles and anoint them, just as He had anointed Jesus. They had to "wait" until they were *"clothed with power from on high"* (Luke 24:49 NASB). At Pentecost, the flow of the Spirit really began (see Acts 2:1-13). Some mockers cried, *"They are full of new wine"* (Acts 2:13). Spiritually, it was true.

Prayer, once again, was the preparation and the driving force of this new wine; also critical to its flow was being in one accord with receiving it (see Acts 1:14, 2:1, 46, 4:24, 5:12, for example).

A flow of miracles began, and, as always, violent opposition immediately followed. Jesus' followers were threatened, but they would not keep quiet. These anointed believers of the early Church quickly learned that they must remain in permanent, violent war mode (see Acts 4:23–5:16). There was no other way to advance the Kingdom.

CHARACTERISTICS OF AN EFFECTIVE WARRING CHURCH (ACTS 4:23-37)

There are several characteristics which must be present in an effective warring church. They are as follows:

1) Great Corporate Prayer Life—Effective One Accord Praying

- It starts with effective "personal" prayers in your "secret place" (see Matt. 6:6).

- Increased power is found in praying in agreement with others (see Matt. 18:19-20).

- The unity of being in one accord in the Spirit with fellow believers creates an atmosphere of faith that cannot be denied (Acts 1:14, 2:1, 2:46, 4:24-34, for example).

The upper room powerhouse was the driving force of this in the early Church, and it became like David's tabernacle.

2) Great Boldness and Mighty Signs and Wonders

These were accomplished because of the anointing that came through continual prayer.

3) Great Power Manifested, Particularly Through the Apostles (Acts 4:33, 5:12)

We must understand the place and role of genuine apostolic authority in the flow of the new wine and receive it joyfully.

4) Living in the Power of the Resurrection

All the power and authority in Heaven and on earth that had been given to Jesus was flowing through His disciples.

5) Great Grace Upon the Whole Church (Acts 4:31-34)

Like the early Church, we must understand the full power of God's grace toward us. This grace was not just to save us, but to empower and transform us. We must learn how to live as constant beneficiaries of that grace and constantly draw on the vast resources of God's grace by faith.

Some brief scriptural examples of the resources of God's grace are listed below. To fully develop them all would require another entire book. So I suggest you prayerfully study each one until you have successfully appropriated this dimension of God's grace in your own life. Some resources of God's grace are:

1. Saving grace (see Eph. 2:7-10)

2. Life-transforming grace (see Gal. 1:15-16; Titus 2:11-14)

3. Grace to go from babes to mature sons and daughters (see Gal. 4:1-7)

4. Grace to go even further and become a *neaniskoi*, which means "strong warrior" (see 1 John 2:12-14)[2]

5. Empowering grace (see 1 Cor. 15:10)

6. Equipping/functioning grace (see Col. 1:28-29; Eph. 3:8)

7. Resurrection/ruling grace (see Eph. 2:5-6)

8. Prospering/enriching grace (see 2 Cor. 9:8)

6) No Needy People Among Them (Acts 4:34)

When the new wine of God's mighty presence came to the early Church, we read that there was not one needy person left. This was expressed in financial terms as well as healings and in every other way. This prosperity flowed out as part of the new wine, which also produced a purity of life including a righteous concern that the Church's financial resources were being properly handled. Land and houses, which people owned and that were surplus to their individual family needs, were sold to provide for the essential needs of others.

Some in the Church obviously had adequate financial resources over and above their own needs, and there were others who were in genuine need. The Church did not leave them in that needy condition, but gave each one an opportunity to come into God's prosperity.

This worked successfully only because:

1. The highest standards of financial integrity were demonstrated on the part of every individual.

2. A healthy Kingdom work ethic had been built into the lives of all the people; no one was allowed to be lazy and exploit the generosity of others.

3. There was purity, honesty, and integrity on the part of everybody, especially in financial matters.

4. Liars, con men, and hypocrites were not tolerated. If anyone tried to come in and pollute the atmosphere, they were very severely dealt with by God and the Church's leaders. In these circumstances, God's severe judgment of Ananias and Sapphira's deceitfulness and hypocrisy (see Acts 5:1-11) is more understandable. It was necessary to maintain this high standard of purity and honesty within the Body of Christ. After that severe judgment, even greater power and miracles flowed

out from the Church, resulting in multitudes being added to the Lord (see Acts 5:12-16).

VIOLENT OPPOSITION DID NOT STOP CHURCH GROWTH

Even beatings or prison did not stop these passionate and courageous believers. The new wine of the Kingdom was not like "John the Baptist Christianity." The persecuted and suffering saints didn't go into depression and doubt in jail. They just continued rejoicing and praised their way out of prison.

The apostles were again imprisoned, threatened, and beaten (see Acts 5:17-42), but as the Church prayed, God sent an angel, and the apostles were miraculously set free. They went straight back to the temple and continued preaching. The Roman soldiers respectfully brought them before the Council again, and they were commanded not to teach in the name of Jesus anymore. However, Peter boldly refused to obey and said to the High Priest, *"We must obey God rather than men"* (Acts 5:29).

After some wise advice from Gamaliel, a respected older scribe who had been Paul's teacher in his student days and who had come to believe secretly in Jesus, the Council decided to only beat them and let them go (see Acts 5:34-40). In the final verses of Acts chapter 5, they rejoiced at being counted worthy to suffer shame for His name, and we read: *"And daily in the temple, and in every house, they did not cease teaching and preaching Jesus as the Christ"* (Acts 5:42).

STEPHEN'S MARTYRDOM SPARKS CHURCH EXPANSION

When Stephen was martyred, even more violent persecution broke out, and the Church in Jerusalem was scattered everywhere. However, the apostles remained together in Jerusalem (see Acts 8:1).

Through Stephen's dying plea for his assailants' forgiveness and the apostles' prayers, suddenly, Saul "saw the light" and was gloriously saved (see Acts 9:1-19), the persecution stopped in three regions, and the Church suddenly had rest and multiplied. Acts 9:31 says:

> *Then the churches throughout all Judea, Galilee, and Samaria had peace and were edified. And walking in the fear of the Lord and in the comfort of the Holy Spirit, they were multiplied.*

The new wine immediately broke forth upon the Gentile world (see Acts 10) with the disciples scattered everywhere. Through the inflow of the Gentiles, the last remains of the old wineskin were finally removed. In Acts 11–15, as the new believing Gentiles poured into the Church, the last remnants of the old wineskin were threatened. After a heated debate in Acts 15, they were finally removed to let the new wine of the Kingdom be contained in a totally new wineskin, which allowed this new wine to flow with freedom and flexibility.

GENTILE LIBERATION SETS THE JEWS FREE

This tide of pressure from the new Gentile believers also set many Jews free. They ceased to practice the unbiblical traditions and laws imposed on them by the scribes and Pharisees based on the oral laws of the Talmud, which were not written in the Torah, the actual Old Testament Scriptures.

Many things changed. At this point, women such as Phoebe and Junia were now given freedom to take their place alongside the men.

Also, when the Gospel of the Kingdom was preached to Jews who did not yet believe, it was still preached with a culturally sympathetic presentation, but it did not compromise the truth that Jesus was their Messiah, King, and Lord, and was the only Savior of the world and the only true God. When they reached the Gentiles, they became "as one of them" without crossing the line of biblical standards of morality, truth, and purity. (See Acts 21:15-25; 1 Cor. 9:19-22.)

Paul was set free as an heir of Christ and began to live unencumbered by the law (see Gal. 4:4-12). He sternly warned the Gentile converts not to be persuaded by those who wanted to make them outwardly into Jews and get them circumcised and then get them into the bondage of keeping the Jewish Law. Paul insisted that these new Gentile believers must stay free in the liberty in which Christ had set them free and not be subject to the yoke of bondage. Paul said to them, "I have become free like one of you Gentiles who never knew the law. Now you must become like me and not be encumbered by it" (see Gal. 4:12).

THE NEW WINESKIN—ITS ESSENTIAL ELEMENTS

The foundation and flow of the new wine is a living relationship with God the Spirit, God the Father, and God the Son. It is not a rule book. It is the fulfillment of all that Jesus taught the disciples from John 14:1 through 17:26.

Every precept of this wonderful discourse needs to be studied and prayed over until it becomes part of each one of us. Jewish believers, in particular, must comprehend the New Covenant as described in Hebrews 8:8-13, realizing that it made the old Mosaic Covenant obsolete, and fully grasping its power for both Jew and Gentile. The Abrahamic Covenant preceded the Mosaic Covenant by hundreds of years, and we must learn to live like Abraham—as friends of God in intimate communion with the Father, Son, and Holy Spirit, as described in John 14:11-23 and as part of a living priesthood under Melchizedek, our glorious High Priest the Lord Jesus Christ. (See Heb. 7:1-3, 14-17; 1 Pet. 2:9.)

The essential elements of the new wineskin, or New Covenant, are summarized below. Each new wineskin believer must continually receive grace to be filled with the life of God and reject living by the rules and regulations of denominational law that are allegedly deduced from the Scriptures. Instead, each of us must:

1. Maintain a deep, intimate, personal relationship with God and soak in a daily, deep experience of the Father's love. We must

really come to know the Father just like Jesus did, just as He had promised. (See John 14:8-11, 16:23-28.)

2. Practice a joyful, willing obedience to all His will because of that love. Jesus said, *"If you love Me, keep My commandments"* (John 14:15). His only question to Peter after His resurrection was: *"Simon, son of Jonah, do you love* [agapao][3] *Me?"* (John 21:16).

3. Be able to "hear" and "see" God in the Spirit and obey His voice in all things, just like Jesus did.

4. Be flexible, ready to move, and ready to change as God directs.

5. Submit to apostolic leaders who are filled with boldness and serve without fear.

6. Become part of a Gideon-hearted company who is also not afraid and ready to follow their leaders all the way.

This kind of "remnant company" biblically and historically has always been a small minority group that is a part of a much larger community of God's people. The majority, even though they are disciples in some measure, has always tended to be more fearful, not so clear-cut, and generally much more passive.

The leaders of such a "remnant" must be warrior apostles leading a powerful spiritual commando group committed to win the war and defeat every enemy that stands in the way of the advancement of God's Kingdom.

In almost every case, both in the Old and New Testaments, this type of company only lasted one generation. The company that had loyally followed such leaders usually vanished when their leader passed away, as in the cases of Moses, Joshua, Gideon, Deborah, and David, for example. There was no successful generational transmission. The next generation always failed to maintain what the previous generation's leaders had established.

May this new Kingdom generation be a glorious exception!

THE TRUE PURPOSE OF RESTORATION

About 30 years after Pentecost, satan initiated a master plan to attack the apostolic leadership of the early Church, so that it was largely destroyed by imprisonment and martyrdom. This lack of apostolic leadership was probably exacerbated by the fact that young apostles were not being recognized, trained, and released as quickly as they should have been by the established apostles.

As a result, a whole generation of the Church between approximately A.D. 60 and A.D. 95 lived without recognized apostolic leadership. During this period, because of severe persecution, the churches generally retreated into survival mode and ceased to be warring, growing churches.

Through lack of apostolic leadership, they became isolated local churches invaded by many demonic assaults including doctrinal error and splits; sadly, they were unable to continue advancing the Kingdom.

APOSTOLIC LEADERSHIP RESTORED

When apostolic leadership was restored, the new wine could flow again within a suitable new wineskin

As we have already seen, God preserved the lone apostle John into his old age. By his inspired writing and by his intensive fathering and discipleship ministry after his release from prison on Patmos, he was able to bring forth a new generation of young apostles, such as Polycarp, Ignatius, and many others mentioned in the writings of the early Church fathers. These new apostolic leaders successfully led that mighty spiritual attack against the stronghold of Diana in Ephesus and liberated the city, as we have already seen.

These same apostolic leaders then pursued a vigorous strategic war against other demonic strongholds in Europe, which all fell one by one. There was a breaking forth of mighty signs and wonders, plus many healings, and the Church was able once again to forcefully advance the Kingdom against all opposition.

This finally brought the Roman Empire to its knees and cleansed Europe from the worship of other gods. Eventually, Jesus was acknowledged as God and Savior, and His Kingdom began to be established everywhere in Europe.

RESPONDING TO CRUCIAL DAYS FOR THE NATIONS

Today, we live in perilous times of great change. It is critical that we be prepared to utilize the weapons God has given us *and* implement the strategies of spiritual warfare revealed to us by the Spirit through prayer and God's Word.

To prepare for the ushering in and advancing of the Kingdom of God in our day, we must seek out others who are of the same heart and spirit; we must become part of a community of warring intercessors in our region. Together we must cry out to God to fully restore the true role of the apostolic ministry, which is to father the Church and make disciples for Jesus. It is imperative that we build again under true apostolic leadership as it was in the early Church and at various times throughout Church history. For this to be most effective, we must pray that these apostles come together in plurality and in full partnership with the prophets so as to give the Church the true biblical foundation described in Ephesians 2:19-22. This is desperately needed, as is the joining of these apostles and prophets with all the other Ephesians 4:11 ministries of evangelists, pastors, and teachers.

As this is accomplished, we will be enabled to raise up city churches in strategic places in our nation. These churches will grow supernaturally like great mustard trees and give shade and protection to our cities and local churches. We will also be able to establish dedicated regional equipping centers of prayer, worship, and spiritual warfare. These will provide resources and an army of warriors to strategically attack and destroy the devil's strongholds in the heavens over our cities and throughout the nations.

It is time to pray like never before and ask God for a mighty flow of the new wine to pour out across our nation in the form of a powerful, fresh anointing of the Holy Spirit. Then the Church must be ready and willing for a flexible, new wineskin to be formed and specifically designed by the Holy Spirit to be suitable for our particular needs and culture at this ordained time. This will facilitate a mighty evangelistic thrust for the redemption of the lost in our nation and throughout the world.

We must all jump in the river of God and let our gifts create a great flow of signs, wonders, and miracles; we must join together with many different people who have each paid the price to be harvesters of precious souls. These souls will be reaped for the glory of God in Jesus' mighty name.

We must pursue the redemption of the "gates" that we have discussed in this book and pray that God's will is increasingly done in our earthly cities just as it is in Heaven. Now more than ever, we must courageously stand in the face of the inevitable opposition that arises in our day, and we must defeat every foul and devious means it uses to stem the flow of this mighty new wine and the advance of God's Kingdom. We must learn the lessons of old and respond like the early Church leaders with joyful praise and unshakable faith, refusing to stop preaching in the mighty name of Jesus, no matter what the penalty might be.

As these things unfold, we can expect an increase in powerful miracles that will bear witness to the truth of the Word being preached and an increase in mighty signs to vindicate the people of God, as it was in the days of the early Church apostles.

May our cry be: *"Lord, it's time for Your Kingdom to fully come on Earth as You promised. Lord, it's time for Your will to be done on earth as it is in Heaven. May Your Kingdom come quickly, and may it fill the whole earth with Your glory, in Jesus' mighty name. Amen!"*

ENDNOTES

1. Alan Vincent, *The Good Fight of Faith* (Shippensburg, PA: Destiny Image Publishers, 2008).

2. *Young's Analytical Concordance,* 1084 (paragraph 21), 942 (paragraphs 31-32).

3. *Biblesoft's New Exhaustive Strong's Numbers and Concordance with Expanded Greek-Hebrew Dictionary.* CD-ROM. Biblesoft, Inc. and International Bible Translators, Inc. (© 1994, 2003, 2006), s.v. "Agapao," (NT 25).

APPENDIX A

THE CITY CHURCH

THE organizational characteristics of a fully developed city church would be as follows:

1. Apostles lead the city church spiritually and direct the strategy and prayer for the church, the region, the nation, and the nations of the world.

2. Elders serve the people and are responsible to shepherd them, bring them to maturity, and lead them into fulfilling the apostolic vision. In each city church there is one clear, consultative head, usually called the senior pastor, who leads the elders and carries final executive authority concerning the city church.

3. Deacons have charge of specific tasks and serve the apostles in the wider work of God or the elders in the city church in a variety of ways.

4. A family atmosphere is developed through congregations and effective home groups.

5. Pastoral care is properly developed through the effective working of the Ephesians 4:11 pastoral ministry.

6. A powerful and effective prayer life is essential and encouraged.

7. An effective evangelistic program is established.

8. Great Sunday celebration meetings are held in which the power of God is present; these meetings draw and feed the people.

9. Steadily growing numbers should be in evidence.

10. A good teaching program is established that is separate from the Sunday preaching for the various levels of maturity and need.

11. An anointed and gifted music ministry results in excellent praise and worship.

12. A youth program effectively ministers to the youth of the church and the region.

13. An effective children's ministry ministers to the children of the church and the region.

14. A strong financial base is created, with all the people released into generous, joyful, faith-filled giving.

15. An effective missions strategy and program is developed to reach the city, the nation, and the nations of the world.

16. An effective method is employed to identify, train, and develop leaders who are put to work in the church, the region, and in missions.

17. The city church is a working body in which every member, both male and female, has found a fulfilling function within that body.

18. Skilled program planning serves the region with conferences, seminars, and specialized visiting ministries that cause the growth and development of the related churches in the region, generally blessing the whole Body of Christ.

19. The necessary buildings and facilities are established to house all of these functions.

Appendix B

Qualities and Functions of a Local Church Within the City Church

WE can summarize these qualities in the following points:

1. A strong sense of local family life should be exhibited in the congregation.

2. People should know each other by name and have real relationships in an atmosphere of helping, teaching, and serving one another.

3. Small things—Jack's new job, Bill's new car, Mary's new baby, and Julie's wedding—should matter.

4. Daily life is overseen by local elders who:

   👑 Bring wise counsel

   👑 Settle small disputes

♛ Supervise pastoral care

5. These elders would concentrate on foundational teaching in areas such as:

♛ New believers' classes

♛ New members' classes

♛ Water baptism

♛ Baptism in the Holy Spirit

♛ How to develop an effective personal life with God

♛ How to hear the voice of God and obey Him

♛ How to participate effectively in the corporate prayer life

♛ Moving in the gifts of the Spirit

♛ Living in financial sufficiency with no debt and plenty to give away

♛ How to study the Bible deeply

♛ Expository teaching of whole books of the Bible

♛ Foundational doctrine—Kingdom family life.

♛ Marriage relationships

♛ Promoting moral purity in teens

♛ Aspects of practical holy living

♛ The keys to victorious Christian living

♕ Coming to Christian maturity and learning to live like Jesus

6. The local elders would also conduct baby dedications, weddings, and funerals and attend to other "family" matters within their own local churches.

7. The local elders would also be responsible for the following:

♕ Prayerfully watching over the spiritual climate of their immediate locality and not allowing any damaging, demonic influence to be established and then remain there unchallenged.

♕ Take the apostolic teaching and the prophetic ministry and work them out on a practical level among the people.

♕ "Envision" the people for world missions and work with the apostles to give the right practical outlets for people to get involved.

8. The elders are not to be responsible for initiating new teaching or deciding the doctrinal policy of the church. These are set by the apostles in association with the prophets and teachers. The elder's job is to adhere to the doctrine of the apostles and teach it faithfully to the people (see Acts 2:42; Titus 1:9).

9. Each congregation or local church when it is fully formed would have a plurality of elders, but always one lead elder or spiritual father of each community usually called the senior pastor or senior elder.

10. The lead elder of each local church congregation sits in the council of the city church with the apostles, prophets, and other Ephesians 4:11 ministries.

11. A vigorous local prayer life is to be embodied in each of the congregations.

12. Local evangelism would go out from each congregation, much of it through individual witnessing and evangelizing through the home groups.

13. The local congregational meetings provide opportunities for gifts and ministry to function and develop at that level.

ABOUT ALAN VINCENT

A LAN VINCENT is an anointed veteran of the faith known as an apostolic father, revelatory, and prophetic teacher of leaders in many nations. His teaching builds and establishes church networks, and inspires believers to activate their faith for huge things. Originally from England, he lived and pioneered in India before coming to the U.S.A.

IN THE RIGHT HANDS, THIS BOOK WILL CHANGE LIVES!

Most of the people who need this message will not be looking for this book. To change their lives, you need to put a copy of this book in their hands.

> *But others (seeds) fell into good ground, and brought forth fruit, some a hundred-fold, some sixty-fold, some thirty-fold* (Matthew 13:8).

Our ministry is constantly seeking methods to find the good ground, the people who need this anointed message to change their lives. Will you help us reach these people?

> *Remember this—a farmer who plants only a few seeds will get a small crop. But the one who plants generously will get a generous crop* (2 Corinthians 9:6).

EXTEND THIS MINISTRY BY SOWING
3 BOOKS, 5 BOOKS, 10 BOOKS, OR MORE TODAY,
AND BECOME A LIFE CHANGER!

Thank you,

Don Nori Sr., Founder
Destiny Image
Since 1982

DESTINY IMAGE PUBLISHERS, INC.

"Promoting Inspired Lives."

VISIT OUR NEW SITE HOME AT
WWW.DESTINYIMAGE.COM

FREE SUBSCRIPTION TO DI NEWSLETTER

Receive free unpublished articles by top DI authors, exclusive
discounts, and free downloads from our best and newest books.

Visit www.destinyimage.com to subscribe.

Write to: Destiny Image
              P.O. Box 310
              Shippensburg, PA 17257-0310

Call: 1-800-722-6774

Email: orders@destinyimage.com

For a complete list of our titles or to place an order
online, visit www.destinyimage.com.

FIND US ON FACEBOOK OR FOLLOW US ON TWITTER.

www.facebook.com/destinyimage   facebook
www.twitter.com/destinyimage   twitter